10 Ambassadors
to
Costa Rica

Thecla E. McCarthy

PublishAmerica
Baltimore

First printing

ISBN: 1-4137-9384-3
PUBLISHED BY PUBLISHAMERICA, LLLP
www.publishamerica.com
Baltimore

Printed in the United States of America

Dedicated to

The Holy Family, Jesus, Mary, and Joseph

Acknowledgments

Terry McCarthy, Sr. and Terry McCarthy, Jr.
My computer consultants

Penny Porter
My mentor and friend

Sue McCarthy and Dorothy Swanson
My readers

My Family
They made it all possible

Secular Franciscans
My spiritual family

Front and Back Cover
Designed by
Joshua McCarthy
My grandson

Contents

Introduction

The letter we received in July of 1964 changed our lives as we knew it. It gave us the chance to accomplish what we dreamed of doing as a family and it opened new and interesting facets to be explored.

It started earlier that year when my husband, Terry, went through the mail one winter day. I came up from the basement with a load of dry clothes.

"Damn it, Mother, I've found just what we have been looking for!"

I read the article in the *Franciscan Herald* magazine that he handed me.

"Gosh, it's exactly what we have in mind"

"They're looking for men to train heavy equipment operators and mechanics for a project in Peru. Could there be anything better than that?"

"That's a perfect description of what we want to do."

By nature, we took changes in stride, and now with our house paid off, we were ready to go again, this time to share with families in foreign lands: We could work hand in hand with them. People and families are always on the move escaping wars, oppression, and injustices. These people move under duress, force, to find freedom, and to remain free: Why not voluntarily move to help prevent war and poverty? A family has so many advantages over single people. The instructors would be working with men with families; these men could more easily identify with instructors who also have families. Would we be able to fulfill our dream? We wouldn't know unless we tried it, so we were on our way.

9

Terry and I met in Petoskey, Michigan in December of 1948. I started to work as secretary in the parish church there a month earlier. He walked into the office just as a couple left with their newly signed marriage certificate.

"Those poor people; they don't know what they're getting into."

Mm, here's a sarcastic one.

"Been there or almost been there?"

"Neither, and I never intend to be."

He had a very self-assured look about him. I noticed his rather unusual headgear (which I later learned was made from an Alaskan hair seal). I looked into his very large blue eyes and handsome, ruddy-complexioned face.

"What can I do for you?"

"I came to say hello to Father Hugolinus; I want to let him know that I am back from Alaska for a short visit with my Mother."

I called Father on the intercom.

"What did you do in Alaska?"

"I worked for the Alaska Railroad: We built a bridge over a canyon, and I operated the crane setting the steel for the bridge."

So this must be the Terry McCarthy I noticed while I posted the Sunday collection in the book. I saw the blank spaces after his name for a long period of time after they had been posted every week before. When I noticed this at the time, I asked Father what had happened to him.

"He belonged to our Youth Group here and sang in the choir for some time, but then he left to work in Alaska."

He was talking with Father now in the office across the hall. As he started to leave, I heard Father say, "Terry, as long as you will be here for a while before you go to South America to work, you might just as well come and sing in the choir again and come to the Youth meetings."

"I might just do that; good-bye, Father."

Several days later, he did come to choir rehearsal. I sat behind him admiring the back of his head of very black hair: a very interesting person. I was tempted to accidentally poke my music sheet onto the back of his neck. After rehearsal, my friend, Elizabeth, and I walked down the hall. Terry came up behind us.

"Where are you going?"

"Anywhere you're going." I couldn't believe I said that; I never said anything like that before to someone I didn't really know; but that is what I did from then on: We were always together.

Petoskey is a beautiful city on the shore of the Little Traverse Bay of Lake Michigan; I spent some summer vacations there with my family. We knew the pastor of the Franciscan Church in Petoskey: He served in our parish in Missouri for quite a while.

On a summer visit, Father Hugolinus said to me, "We need to hire a secretary because of the growth of our parish: Would you like to work here? I would really like to start out with someone who doesn't know the parishioners well."

Mm, leave my work at Capitol Records and live here?

"I'll think about it, Father."

I returned to work at Capitol Records Distributing House in St. Louis. There, I started taking notice of the large turnover of the people working with me: here today, gone tomorrow. I received a gold pin for my first anniversary of work there: some indication of the turnover. I liked the work I did, but after a few weeks I decided that working for the parish in Petoskey presented a challenge much more satisfying.

I called Father one day. "I accept your offer, Father. I'm looking forward to seeing the beauty of the winter in Petoskey." Three weeks later I rode the train from St. Louis to Petoskey via Chicago.

Talk about the Irresistible Force meeting the Immovable Object— this was it! I came from the recording business in St. Louis; he from building a railroad bridge in Alaska for a pause in Petoskey to visit his mother before going to South America to work. Together we watched the waves of the bay, so gentle in the summer, now crashing onto the dock. We watched the bay slowly fill in with ice. We went to the "Winter Sports Ball." (The Governor, G. Mennen Williams, also attended.) During all this time, I never heard any word from Terry about going to

South America to work.

Instead, he went to work in the boiler room of "The City of Cheboygan," a ferry that carried cars and passengers across the Straits of Mackinac between Lake Michigan and Lake Huron. Terry stopped by the office on his way to work on the Straits one day.

"Why don't you come up Sunday and take the trip across the Straits on my last shift?"

"Wow, that would be great! I'd love to do that."

That Sunday, as I parked the car in the lot by the ferry dock in Macinac City, I couldn't believe the change in the Straits: In the summer, the blue of the water defied description; now dark, gray, choppy waves greeted me. I watched the ferry come in to the dock. The ramp which enables the cars and trucks to load and unload onto the ferry was in place, but at the last minute a wave tossed the ferry up, and as it came down again, the ramp dropped with a loud bang onto the dock. Before the ferry could be secured, another wave came and the process was repeated. After several attempts, the ferry finally was in place at the dock.

Terry met me on deck and took me down to the boiler room; I watched the fireman shoveling coal into the firebox of the boiler. From there, we went into the engine room. I'm usually not bothered with motion sickness, but now the ferry rocked from side to side and the engine connecting rods went up and down, and that spelled trouble.

"Terry, I'm going up on deck right now."

"Okay, I'll see you up there a little later."

When I got outside into the cold air, the nausea left. I loved the feel of the wind in my face; the gulls looked so different flying against the gray clouds now instead of the blue summer sky.

At lunch time, Terry came back on deck. "Do you feel like coming inside for lunch?"

"That sounds great to me."

We went inside the cabin and I noticed the table cloths were wetted down to hold the plates in place; a wooden rim on the edge of the table gave extra protection. I enjoyed a T-bone steak with all the trimmings.

When the ice took over the water in the Straits, Terry transferred to the railroad ferry, "The Santa Maria." The Coast Guard ice breaker cleared a channel in the ice; the railroad ferry alone could withstand the chunks of ice floating in the channel. The other ferries were laid up during this time. I drove up to the Straits again to ride the ferry on the last trip across on Terry's shift. He came on deck to meet me.

"I think I'll stand out here in front of the pilot house; I'd like to watch the ferry maneuver in this small channel."

"Okay, but it'll be a cold trip."

As we got underway, the wheelsman broke the ship into the edge of the solid field of ice. It sounded like a rifle shot as the ice split from the main field. I jumped at the sound: That brought smiles to the faces of the men inside the pilot house. I learned later that they keep breaking into the ice field to keep the channel open. It *was* very cold standing on deck, but I enjoyed every bit of it. (I wore Terry's hair seal hat with the flaps over my ears on this trip.) Northern Michigan can be an enchanting place in the winter.

The months passed, and before long I was wearing an engagement ring: A delay in Terry's plan to work in South America was imminent.

Our wedding took place in Petoskey with a Solemn High Mass offered by the priests whom we had known so long: Father Hugolinus, Father Venard and Father Benign. The choir sang the various parts of the Mass. It included the Gloria and Credo because it occurred during the Octave of Corpus Christi— very beautiful. Driving through town after the Mass, we saw flags lining the main streets; no, they were not for us: June 14 is Flag Day.

Our first home was a tiny, third-floor apartment of a beautiful, old, large house across the street from Bear Creek. We could hear the water flow over the dam on its way to Little Traverse Bay. From the window in the living room, we watched the sun set in the middle of the Bay. Petoskey was known as the city of the million dollar sunsets.

We were a good combination of spirits. I found contentment in caring for the children; Terry always looked to other places and things to be accomplished: a nice balance. It kept things interesting. We started our married life by saying our evening prayers together; even when apart, we knew that the other was saying the same evening prayer.

Early on we felt a need for some spiritual direction too. This led us to a lay religious order, the Third Order of St. Francis. It made us part of a worldwide spiritual family. The priests comprise the First Order, the Poor Clare cloistered nuns, the Second Order.

The years in between our marriage and going to pursue our dream, 1950 to 1964, were filled with joys, sorrows, ups and downs: Having a good sense of humor helped a lot. I read somewhere that a real sense of humor is what balances the mysteries of joy and sorrow.

Eleven children were born to us during that time, each one such a treasure. Terry, Jr., 14, came into the world on a snowy, April morning in St. Louis, Missouri; our second home for a while. We then moved to Grand Haven, Michigan. There, a large two-story farm house on one acre of land proved ideal for our third home. Kevin, 12, Rory, 11, Robert, 9, Cronan, 7, Joseph, one day old when he died, Sean, 5, Christopher, 4, Brigid, 2, and Hilary, 1, made up the rest of the McCarthy clan, as did Camille, born in February of 1965. I have never known a greater joy than holding a new-born baby in my arms with the velvet feel of their skin pressed to my lips. While holding them to my breast to feed them, I could say with St. Elizabeth Seton, "I can have all this and heaven too."

As noted above, we had eight boys before our first girl, Brigid, came into the family. Our family doctor, Dr. Stobbelaar, delivered ten of the children.

As he delivered Brigid, he said, "You have a baby girl!"

"Oh, don't kid me, Doctor." Then I looked up and saw the excitement in his face.

"I would never kid you about that when you've been waiting for a girl so long."

He rarely showed any emotion over anything, but by the time I reached my room, everyone in the maternity ward knew we had a girl. The following day, during the noon newscast at the local radio station, our neighbor, Bob Schmitt, announced in the headlines, "The McCarthy family lost their baseball team. They had a girl this time."

As our family grew, I experienced the truth of the statement that the family together is the home no matter where you are. Once when we made a trip to Missouri to see my folks, we decided to go at night so the children could sleep most of the way. With Terry, Jr., Kevin, and Rory already in the car, I took Bob, our fourth son, out of his bed; he snuggled in my arms in his sleep and then stretched out again in the car, sound asleep along with his other brothers. For a short time the car would be our home because we were together and content; we experienced this many times over during that period of years in many different places.

We dealt with a very limited budget since Terry worked with heavy equipment in the gravel pit. It is seasonal work because of the cold Michigan winters. He worked at temporary jobs then. The Mangleson Brothers owned a grocery store near us; if we ran into difficulty, they extended credit to us until we could take care of it—very special people.

Terry wanted a home on wheels to take the family on vacations. One evening, while getting the little children ready for bed, he said, "If I could find a used highway bus, I could convert it into a home for us."

"How are we going to fit *that* into our budget?"

"If I could find a bus boneyard somewhere, I could get an idea if we could afford one. It would mean a lot of work to fix one up, but that's okay."

Several days later he came home with the news. "A mechanic from an equipment company came to the gravel pit today. He told me where I could go to look at busses; they're in a lot near Grand Rapids. I'll check that out Saturday."

Terry, along with Terry, Jr., and Kevin, went to Grand Rapids on Saturday and found the place. The gentleman who owned the lot at one time contracted to bring workers from Mexico to work in the fields in the summer: He took them back to Mexico in the fall. He no longer did that; consequently, he wanted to sell the busses. Terry found one that had a good engine, but the body of the bus left a lot to be desired: The price was right, so he bought it.

We tried it out that summer on a trip to the National Music Camp at Interlochen, Michigan. Terry and I visited the camp years before. Now we wanted our children to enjoy it. Earlier in the year we received a schedule for the summer season at the Music Camp. Kevin was reading it.

"Dad, Howard Hanson is teaching at Interlochen this summer; let's take our album of his Romantic Symphony along and have him autograph it for us."

"That's a good idea, Kevin. I'll put you in charge of seeing that it gets there and back in good condition."

The first afternoon at Interlochen we sat in the open air theater, marveling at the beauty of the pines and the sun sparkling on the lake in back of the stage. The concert began with the *Music Camp Theme* which is from Howard Hanson's *Romantic Symphony*. He conducted the students' orchestra that afternoon. What beauty God lavished on us that day—the talent of the young artists playing the music, the composer, their teacher conducting the music, and the beauty of nature all came together to give us this memorable afternoon. After the concert, Terry, Jr., Kevin, and Rory went to meet Howard Hanson, and he graciously autographed the album.

From Interlochen, we went a little farther north to Petoskey to visit Grandma McCarthy and Aunt Ginny, Terry's sister, and her family. We parked the bus in a picnic area by Little Traverse Bay. Terry and the children were busy looking for "Petoskey Stones," unique stones used in jewelry.

Aunt Ginny drove in to visit us; she inspected our home on wheels, inside and out. "This reminds me of the vehicle in the movie 'Tobacco Road'."

Terry looked over at her as he showed Chris and Brigid a new stone he found.

"We're just checking out the engine performance this trip; we haven't done anything to the interior yet. We'll probably get another body in better shape and work with that."

And that is what he did: He went back to the bus lot and found another bus; this one had a good body but no engine, so he bought it. He came home with the news of what he found.

Rory had a puzzled look on his face. "But, Dad, how will we get this bus home if it has no engine?"

"That's no problem; we'll rent a truck and tow the bus home; my friend, Ray, will help me."

He rented a large truck from a construction contractor; with the help of his friend, he towed the bus home. This was no small accomplishment. The acre lot provided ample room for both busses. My mom and dad came to visit us about that time. We congregated in the back yard. My dad, an automobile mechanic, looked at the two busses.

"Terry, there's no way you can take the engine out of one bus and put it into the other bus by yourself."

"You just don't know Terry, Dad; I'm sure he had it all figured out a long time ago."

Terry smiled and said, "Don't worry, I'll find a way."

He did find a way. The engine was mounted in the rear of the bus; he built a cradle to rest the engine on when he disconnected it from its mountings. As the engine was disconnected, Terry, Terry, Jr., and Kevin lowered the engine and cradle to boards below. Short lengths of pipes, placed between the cradle and the boards, acted as rollers. By re-laying the pipes and repositioning the boards as they went along, they rolled the cradle and engine to the rear of the other bus, a distance of some 30 feet. The rest of the children and I cheered as the engine reached the other bus. The next day they started installing the engine into *that* bus.

We named our bus Troubadour for St. Francis who was known as Christ's Troubadour. We painted it black with white trim and painted the names of the children under each window; the boys and Dad on the driver's side, Mom and the girls on the passenger side. It was not a fair contest, though, since we had eight boys and one girl at that time.

Working in the evenings and any chance he had, Terry dismantled the original interior, experimented with it, and rebuilt it to accommodate the family. The Troubadour had two fold-down tables with recliner seats on either side, a couch, a used gas stove, a chemical toilet, bunk beds to sleep all the children and lots of storage space beneath the bottom bunk beds. It was built mostly of love and determination; we made many wonderful trips in our Troubadour.

On one of the trips, we went to Missouri to visit my folks. On the way back to Grand Haven, we stopped at a gas station a few miles outside of town. A car pulled in alongside us.

A man got out, walked to the front of the bus, looked at the name and then came to the door of the bus. "I told my family, 'if that bus has the name Troubadour on the front, I saw it in Washington, Missouri and I want to see who owns it.'"

I came down the aisle of the bus. "Hello, Doctor Cassidy. Remember me?"

"Hello, Thecla, what a pleasure to see you."

He was a dentist I knew when I still lived at home. I introduced him to our family.

"Congratulations, Terry. You have a wonderful home on wheels: It's very unique."

Now our family was ready to take a much different trip and pursue another way of life: What new things would we learn and experience and enjoy in the next phase of our life?

REMEMBERING

To my husband, Terry
Whose blue Irish eyes can still
make my heart beat faster when they
gaze into mine.
How many years has it been since I
took time to watch your face deep in thought
still eager,
still standing there, straight and tall
with that independent air
I grew to love when we first met.
Didn't I tell you that you're handsome,
that your funny quips cheered me through
the days of diapers, dishes, and drearies,
that your tenderness melted the cold in my heart
when we lost our little ones?

Now I know that all couples must again
and again take the time to look and see
the eyes, the face, the one they first loved.
And so I write this for our love, our children
our grandchildren,
for you, my husband, Terry
and our 55 years, going on five.

Chapter I

Camp Out in Wisconsin

For about three years we had the basic concept of what we wanted to do as a family. During that time, Terry studied the Social Teachings of the Church. These stressed that the first and immediate apostles of the working men must themselves be working men, or perhaps the apostolate of like to like. Likewise, the first apostles among the business and professional people must be business and professional people. This would allow us to then integrate the working people with business and professional people. This calls for operators, who can operate any kind of heavy equipment that will move, to instruct others how to operate that equipment. It calls for mechanics, who can repair and maintain any kind of heavy equipment, to train other mechanics to repair and maintain equipment properly. These operators and mechanics would be able then to integrate this knowledge with road design and other professional skills.

Terry started calling the people involved with the article in the magazine that he showed me that winter day. As he finished, he walked into the kitchen to me with a notepad in his hand, his eyes sparkling.

"I just talked with John Murphy, who will head the project in Peru.

There's quite a story behind it. He has various client companies in the heavy equipment business and travels to South America on field coverage assignments for them; John saw a real need for a training center for operators and mechanics there and he wants to start a center. He…"

"Has John done the research needed for all that?"

"Yeah, he found a center like that is already working in Mexico City. The center really impressed him; he sent his research personnel down there, and they came back to Arlington Heights, Illinois with all the manuals for the courses; their technical services division translated the manuals into English, prepared lists of equipment needed for such a training center, and adapted and adjusted the training courses for use of the instructors they would recruit here: very thorough research."

"Sounds like John covered all the bases."

"Yeah, in Lima, Peru, he talked to a heavy equipment distributor; they arranged a meeting with the Peruvian Highway Association and the Automobile Association officials. They set their goals to provide educational and training facilities for the center; they wanted to work through private channels rather than direct governmental sponsorship."

"Did they come up with contracts for this?"

"Yes, they did. Two not-for-profit corporations emerged: *Centro de Adiestramiento de Mecanicos y Operadores* in Peru (CAMO) and Inter-American Technical Assistance Foundation (ITAF) in the United States. CAMO contracted to secure land, erect buildings and provide student scholarships; ITAF contracted to recruit instructors and provide the necessary equipment for the center."

"So why the article about all of this in the Franciscan magazine? What do they have to do with it?"

"Oh yeah, John's a member of the Third Order Franciscans. He wanted them to take part in it. The Third Order of St. Francis in North America would participate as the Vico Necchi Apostolate, named after an Italian Third Order businessman. Their objective: to insure financial support and to recruit volunteer instructors. At one of the start-off meetings, a note was received from the Papal Nuncio to the US giving the blessings of Pope John XXIII."

"I like that idea of including them in the project. What's their plan for the volunteers who go there?"

"Well, John said the first instructors, after their training here, would go to Peru to train the Peruvian students; then those students instruct the local people in Peru."

"They did their groundwork well; I hope we can take part in it."

"Oh, John said also that Father Philip Marquard, OFM, who was a member of the ITAF board, sent a wire to the Franciscan Cardinal Ricketts, OFM in Peru, to ask his blessing for the Third Order participation in the project: He gave them his blessings."

"I guess we just wait to hear from them now."

"You got that right! John was a little speechless when he heard the size of our family, but he's definitely interested in my qualifications—so we'll see how it goes."

As we waited, Terry made his annual retreat at St. Lazare Retreat House in Spring Lake, Michigan, just a few miles from our home. He talked extensively with the priests there about the project. Everything was indicative to our going. When I made my retreat later on, I received the same encouragement. In all that time, from start to finish, we only heard objections from people we felt did not grasp the spirit or intention of the project. From them we heard you just can't do that.

"Terry can't leave thirteen years of seniority."

"You can't take children off like that."

"What about their education?"

"What will your families think?"

"How much money is there in it?"

"You just can't do that."

Our reply, "Yes, we think we *can* do that."

On a July morning in 1964, Terry went through the mail.

"Mother, we have a letter from ITAF; we'll know in a minute if we're going to Peru!"

I came running into the kitchen as he opened the letter.

"Yes, we're going. I start training for the project in Arlington

Heights, Illinois, in three weeks!"

We hugged each other and knew that now our work began. We informed Terry's employer of his leaving, told our families what we planned to do, and began tying up all the loose ends.

Terry found it difficult to tell the Men's Choir of our plans; he had directed the choir for two years. Two of our sons, Kevin and Rory, sang soprano in it. From singing hymns in unison when he first took over, they now sang in four-part harmony: The sound that came out completely fascinated them. They never sang in Latin before either: Terry had wanted them to learn that, too. He had talked to the Assistant Pastor, Father McKinney, after Mass one Sunday.

"Would you teach the men in the choir how to pronounce Latin?"

Father thought for a while and said, "I could record all the words you need on tape; then the men can learn them by listening to the tape."

"That's a deal, Father." And so the choir began their work with the Latin in preparation for Palm Sunday and Easter.

One evening, Terry finished washing Hilary's face and hands after dinner. He prepared to leave for choir practice.

"How about coming with me tonight? It's our last practice before Palm Sunday; I'd like you to hear us."

"I would love to go. I know I can't go Sunday with the children because the Service is too long; I'll be ready in a minute."

I sat down in the front part of the Church. The practice started with the men singing the Litany of the Saints in Latin; their pronunciation was crisp and clear. As they came down the middle aisle singing *Ingrediente Domino* in harmony, tears streamed down my face. It was so beautiful—only six men were singing, but it sounded as though the roof of the church would lift off. I could hardly believe what they accomplished.

"Congratulations to all of you—it's incredible!"

One Sunday after Mass I talked with Christine Gallagher, the wife of one of the members of the choir; Father McKinney walked over and started talking with us.

Christine said, "Father, it's just a shame that the men wasted all that time singing those parts in Latin: Now they're changing it all into

English."

"Christine, when I heard them singing the first night they started practice, it sounded like a bunch of frogs croaking. What they just did for Palm Sunday and the four-part harmony of the Mass they've completed is an accomplishment they will never forget."

On July 5, 1964, we went to the choir picnic and said our good-byes to all of them.

Driving home, Terry said, "Well, Mother, tomorrow we start an entirely new life; nothing will ever be the same again."

"I know; it certainly presents a challenge, and I'm looking forward to it."

Terry and the other instructors began their training in Arlington Heights; they moved into the apartment John rented for a Peruvian family there. The family consisted of the mother, Rosario, her student son, Fernando, and her daughter, Ana Maria. John met them in Peru on one of his trips there. They were relatives of the construction equipment distributor he knew in Lima. He hired the family to train the instructors. Fernando, then a sophomore at Loyola University in Chicago, combined his own studies with instructing the recruits, Terry, Tom Putzbach, and Wilbur Frankinburger. For several hours each day, he drilled them in the Spanish language. Rosario prepared Peruvian dishes for the men. During the meals, she helped them understand the country in which they would be working. She also gave them some idea what it would be like for them to teach the Peruvians who would be their students. Living together was never an easy thing for anyone. Terry had never been away from the family that much before; his daily physical work now changed to sitting inside through Spanish lessons and working on the programs John brought from Peru, along with getting accustomed to a new culture. However, the experience gained was priceless.

During this training period, Terry took the train into Chicago Sunday evening and came back to Grand Haven Friday night. This left the car with me during the week. Friday became a holiday because Dad came home—Sunday afternoon brought the little ache when he left again. The nights in between were hard. Terry and I did all of our talking about the day's events after the children went to bed. Now, I couldn't tell him that Hilary cut another tooth today and is managing to crawl very well, that Brigid helped me bake bread today: she's so different after all the boys, that Wednesday, Terry and Kevin didn't come home on the school bus—that was quite a tale to tell.

I called the school and learned that both the boys got on the bus at school after classes.

The driver called me a little later. "They got off the bus at the stop before yours: They'll probably come home soon."

"Thank you so much for calling; I don't have any idea why they did that, but I sure appreciate your call."

I could not imagine what prompted the boys to get off the bus there and it upset me. A little later, I received a call from the father of a boy who lived by the stop where Terry and Kevin got off that day.

"Mrs. McCarthy, I guess my son has been giving Terry a bad time on the bus. Terry and Kevin got off the bus here and Terry cleaned my son's clock in front of my house. I watched and so did your son, Kevin. It was a good, clean fight. My son had it coming. Terry and Kevin are walking home, so they'll be there soon."

I was speechless at first but then managed to say, "Thank you for calling—it's very kind of you."

A little while later, they came walking down the road, looking none the worse for wear.

"Well, what do you have to say for yourself?"

Terry said, "Mom, Dad always said we should stand up for what we thought was right. Danny made trouble on the bus every day, and I didn't think it was fair to the bus driver, so I got off with him today to settle it."

"He had it coming, Mom," Kevin added, "Danny's Dad said so, too."

"Okay, let's go in and you can get washed up."

Somehow, I just didn't find time to tell Terry about all these things on the weekends. I considered it part of *my* training, though, because a little later, in a strange country, he'd be gone over long periods of time, too.

John scheduled one week of training, August 14 to 22, for all the people in the project to camp out on a lake in northern Wisconsin. He wanted to test the ability of the family and instructors to live out on their own. This included lack of running water, electricity, and appliances. We were to live with the very basic necessities, something we might have to deal with for a time in Peru.

Early in August we started packing for the campout. Terry, Kevin, Rory, Bob, Cronan, and Sean began to get their clothes together. Cronan looked at the mounting pile.

"Gosh, Mom, what an undertaking; look what we have already, and we still have the other kids' clothes to pack!"

"We always had all the storage space on the bus when we traveled. Now our things need to fit into the suitcases. I'm glad we have the Checker instead of a regular car. That extra room, where the Checker cabs have the jump seats, will help a lot."

With a little pushing and shoving, we did manage to get it done.

We arrived at the apartment in Arlington Heights Friday afternoon and met the other instructors and the Peruvian family. We arrived just in time to take part in celebrating Wilbur's birthday. With the candles lit, the children sang *Happy Birthday* in Spanish for him. That was just about the extent of our knowledge of Spanish at the time. The apartment of the Peruvian family and John's home then absorbed the members of our family, which was no small task.

After an early Mass on Saturday, the feast of the Assumption of the Blessed Virgin Mary, with everyone present and accounted for, we started for Wisconsin. John's station wagon, the project Jeep, and our Checker made up the convoy. At noon, we stopped in a little park to eat a picnic lunch. By mid-afternoon we were nearing our destination. We entered the dense woods on a two-rut road; thank heavens for the extra height of the Checker, for we encountered some pretty rough spots. It appeared as though it had been quite a while since anyone used this road. At one spot we saw the beautiful lake in the distance.

A little further down the road Terry said, "Look what's up ahead on the side of the road. It looks like an old, wood-burning cooking stove."

"What in the world is it doing here in the middle of nowhere? There's no evidence of a house or a cabin anywhere around here."

"I haven't seen one of those in a long time. We might find some use for it, though, before we leave."

We came out of the woods onto a small clearing on the shore of the lake. While everyone set about the job of unpacking, I began to prepare the evening meal. I brought along my trusty 16-quart pressure cooker. Wherever I went, the cooker went too. John saw me use it on different occasions and laughed when he saw me bring it out.

"I've never seen anyone so attached to a cooking utensil. I can picture you crossing the Andes with that faithful cooker under your arm."

"John, I know what this cooker can do to a tough piece of meat in a matter of an hour: It saved many a day for me."

"You'll probably be putting it to good use where you're going to live."

We fired up the gas camp stove and soon we were eating hot slumgullian, a concoction borrowed from Terry's mother: hamburger browned with onions, and then covered with sliced carrots, potatoes, green beans and corn along with tomato juice. It needed to cook only ten minutes with the pressure up.

By nightfall a tent village emerged on the shore of the lake. At the entrance of the village, a berm with the letters ITAF formed from large rocks gave it an official air.

The next morning, after going into town for Mass, we set up a schedule with all the assigned jobs. Terry, Tom, and Wilbur's schedule included daily Spanish lessons. Spanish lessons for the children and me were also included. Going swimming, fishing, canoeing, and playing soccer as part of the day was a foregone conclusion.

The Peruvian family found it very difficult. Their presence here at camp, of course, was voluntary, but they had just come to the States. In their home in Peru, they were accustomed to servants; here at camp they found the complete opposite.

Fernando and Ana Maria, however, began to really enjoy it. Ana Maria got Brigid dressed in the mornings and played with her and Hilary during the day.

"This beats sitting around with white gloves on most of the day. That's what I did at home in Peru. It's so much fun with a little sister to dress in the morning."

"I'm glad you enjoy it, Ana Maria. It helps me a lot, too."

Fernando started teaching the men and the boys to play soccer after he taught the Spanish lessons for the day: He went after it with a passion.

"I never thought I'd be teaching soccer. You're getting too good, though; I'm panting trying to keep up with you."

Bob, catching his breath, said, "You're just too good a teacher, Fernando."

"You're all doing real well for never having played before; I'm really enjoying it."

Rosario, however, found the conditions almost insurmountable. She struggled just to get going in the morning, walking to another tent to get her clothes and toiletries, and using cold water in a basin to wash up. She came through it, though, showing the qualities of the fine woman she was, but I don't think she was ever the same again.

Soccer in Wisconsin

Wisconsin Camp

With Hilary 10 months old, we had the daily diapers to wash. We needed to find a place to set up the washtub.

Cronan said, "Let's set up the tub and scrub board on the tailgate of the Jeep; that looks like a good height for you, Mom."

"Okay, let's try it."

We brought the tub over to the Jeep and placed it on the tailgate: a perfect height. With the water heating on the stove, we were now in the laundry business.

When Rosario and the children and I sat down for our Spanish lesson, she started with a text book, but usually in a short time the book lay open on her lap as she talked about Peru.

"You will see the beautiful ancient buildings in Lima. How I love them."

"I'm sure we will learn to love them, too, Rosario; I really enjoy seeing the old parts of a city."

"You will shop for fruits and vegetables in the market, too; it will be very different from shopping in the supermarkets here."

"That will probably mean I'll spend a lot more time shopping for food there; I'd better take that into consideration."

Sometimes she told us what she did in Lima.

"I was secretary to my uncle, the Second Vice President of Peru. I went to formal dinners in the lovely homes. It was so grand. But we didn't have air conditioning like you do here. Did you ever try to shape your hair while an electric fan blows on you? Believe me, it doesn't work too well."

"I can imagine that's next to impossible."

Then she sadly told of how it felt to come to a strange country and why she came.

"I wanted to be with my children while they studied here."

"I certainly can understand how you feel about that. I would want to do the same."

At times, I could see the longing to return to her country in her blue, Spanish eyes: Her father was English.

Rosario and I did most of the cooking. One of the instructors assisted us at each meal. The older boys took turns doing the dishes and cleaning up after the meal.

One day Rosario announced, "I will make tortillas for breakfast tomorrow, so this afternoon I will cook the potatoes for the tortillas."

Potatoes for tortillas? That's quite different!

The next morning I awoke to find Tom beating eggs in a bowl with a whisk. "Why are you doing that, Tom?"

"It's for the tortillas that Rosario is making for breakfast."

The eggs were mixed with the finely cut potatoes along with some spices; then portions of the mixture poured into a very hot skillet and fried.

"This is much different than any tortillas we have here, Rosario; it's more like our omelets."

"We serve them many times for breakfast in Peru, especially for the working men."

"They are delicious, Rosario."

With the number of people at camp, quite a few batches were made to feed everyone. I can still see Tom standing there, displaying the stiff arm he acquired from beating all the eggs.

Another day, Rosario made a delicious sauce which she served over cooked kidneys: She was a superb cook.

"Rosario, how did you learn to cook when you always had servants in the house?"

"All the girls are taught the homemaking skills even though we have servants: You never know when you'll have to use them; I surely need those skills now."

All during the week, after lessons and chores, some went fishing, others swimming, still others canoeing or playing soccer. Fernando was a good soccer instructor, proven by the fierce competition in the games played.

Christopher became quite attached to Tom during that week. At free time, Tom always looked for him. "There's my main man."

"I really like you, Tom. I'm going to miss you when we go home."

When we returned home after the campout, Chris found a turtle down by the channel of the river near our home. He came running home with the turtle with the announcement, "This is Tommy the turtle; I named him for Tom."

I brought along two quarts of green tomato mince meat which I canned at home. This recipe was another borrowed from Terry's mother, Minnie. Our family just loved pies made of it.

About the middle of the week, Terry said, "I'm going over to that old cook stove we saw when we came here and start a fire in it; some mince meat pies sound awfully good to me right now."

"I forgot to bring a rolling pin along but I guess I can find a replacement."

"I'm sure you'll find something."

I browned a big roast, put it under pressure in my cooker, and then started making pie crusts. I found a large enough space, fairly smooth, to roll out the dough; then I searched for a replacement for the rolling pin. A bottle of cooking wine Rosario brought worked quite well. The crusts were unique: Each one had the raised letters of the logo on the face of the bottle on it.

Terry returned as I finished the pies. "The fire is going good and I think it'll stay hot long enough to bake the pies."

"Okay, I'll go and try my hand at using a stove I've only seen my Grandma use when I was young."

Arriving at the spot, I opened the oven door, which probably hadn't been touched in years, and a huge spider, the size of a tarantula, dislodged itself from the rim of the door. He seemed quite anxious to escape the heat, but not nearly as anxious as I was to be rid of him. He sailed by my head as I jerked to the side: That shook me up for a while. I placed the pies in the oven and started exploring the woods: a beautiful and peaceful place. Then I sat back in my chair and enjoyed looking at the lake.

When I checked the pies, I noticed the top crust browned nicely but the bottom crust looked quite pale through the Pyrex dish. I took them out of the oven and set them on the burner covers on top of the stove to brown the bottom crusts: That did the trick.

I had quite a following as I arrived back at camp. Everyone smelled the freshly baked pies and came to look at them. They were a welcome dessert.

In the evenings, we built a big fire. Everyone in camp gathered around, and the singing started: What a variety of songs there were.

Ana Maria sang the songs from *West Side Story*; she loved the song, "Maria,"and said, "I wish my name was just Maria instead of Ana Maria, and someone was singing that song to me."

Rosario sang lullabies to Hilary in Spanish. One of them he really liked was "Cinco Los Lobos," which was like our, " This Little Piggy," where you use each of the five fingers for a piggy. When she said good night to him, he would wiggle his five fingers: She really laughed then.

Tom and Wilbur tried to sing some songs in Spanish and had everyone roaring with laughter: Their pronunciation of the words was quite unique.

After the children went to bed, some discussions were held by the rest of us: They were quite interesting.

At first, Rosario said to me, "There is no way you can take the children on such a project. It's just too hard for the mother and the children."

"Rosario, our children are accustomed to working together. I think you'll notice that as we go along."

We talked about education for the children, the climate of the area where we would be located, how the shopping would be done and about the availability of medical attention. As the week progressed, Rosario seemed to be changing her mind about how our family would fare in Peru.

Friday, she came to me as I washed diapers. "I know your family will thrive anywhere you go. I've been watching the children; they know what is expected of them and they do it: They're very mature."

"Thank you, Rosario, I'm glad you agree."

Mother Nature joined in our venture and gave us just about

everything in the line of weather that one could encounter. We had swimming days, fishing days, and canoeing days. One morning we awoke to find everything shimmering with a coat of frost. Then the rain came: rain, rain, rain, and more rain. The rear of the jeep now held the gas stove.

Terry looked at his forlorn group huddled in the tent and said, "How would you like a nice hot bath?"

"That's not funny, Dad; how are we going to do that?"

"Just you wait and see," and off he went.

Soon curiosity got the better of the older boys, and they disappeared from the tent.

They came back laughing and Rory said, "Wait and see what Dad's doing."

Soon Terry appeared at the entrance of our tent with towel in hand. "Your bath awaits you."

He escorted me out to one of the other tents; he had transformed it into a bathhouse. The washtub steamed with hot water and served as the bathtub. The jeep, backed up to the tent, held buckets of water heating on the stove for the next bath: This was heavenly.

"You never cease to amaze me; what a wonderful Dad."

Saturday, August 22, our son Bob's birthday, and we headed back to Arlington Heights; John preceded us earlier in the week. Rose had dinner ready when we arrived at their house: meat loaf, baked beans, salad, and cake for dessert.

"Oh, Rose, I don't think I've ever smelled anything so good."

"I thought you would be ready to sit down and eat when you came back."

She quickly transformed the cake for dessert into a birthday cake for Bob: It turned into a festive occasion.

We returned to Grand Haven. Terry went back to Arlington Heights on Monday. The pears on the little tree in our back yard were ripe and waiting to be canned. As I sat preparing them for canning, I had time to meditate and evaluate our progress as a family in the project: I saw no major problems. Even though Terry spent much of the time away from home during the training period, there were still close ties.

During the campout, the family got along fine under those living conditions. The boys handled all the jobs well. They stayed with the little one they were paired with and we never had to worry about them. I was pregnant at the time, but I also made out just fine with no ill effects at all.

However, living at camp with Rosario, Fernando, and Ana Maria brought out some direct opposites in thinking that sort of made me wonder about going to Peru to live. They were very class conscious, and I wasn't used to that. I knew that there was a lot of difference in cultures, but I didn't know if I could handle that part of it. The children accepted them and didn't have any problems. So it brought out that it was the adults and not the children who had the difficulty.

Time slipped by, and Terry and the other instructors made a special retreat at the Trappist Retreat House at Gethsemani, Kentucky. The priest who gave the conferences was very firm and positive and said a number of times, "You boys are on the right track, but you'll have to bull your way through some of the things that are ahead for you."

A few weeks later, Terry came home early so I could make a weekend retreat. I had a long talk with Father McQuillan regarding the questions I had about living in Peru.

"I know you quite well, Thecla, and I don't think you'll have a problem with that."

"Okay, Father, I'll go along with that."

So we moved on with our dream.

Chapter II

Cold, Silent Winter

November came, and we made plans for Thanksgiving. Terry's sister, Dolores, her husband, Gerri, and family, lived on a 60-acre farm near Kent City, Michigan, about 40 miles from our home. She invited us to their home for dinner. We always had a ball when we got together. It was our favorite place for visiting. Their children, Mary, Tim, Mark, Patricia, Kristine, Michael, Stephen, and Joseph paired off with ours so we had two of each age right on down the line.

On the way to the farm, the children discussed what they'd do when we got there; most of the conversation dealt with all the good things to eat. Dolores was a marvelous cook and always had every conceivable type of relishes and pickles, besides all the canned vegetables from her garden.

I brought along pumpkin pies; she would have the mince meat pies. She and I both used her Mother's recipe of green tomato mince meat. Most of the food was ready when we arrived. There's nothing quite like the wonderful aroma of a Thanksgiving dinner. The children paired off and Dolores and I engaged in a good gab fest while we worked on the last minute preparations.

When all was ready we filled the plates for the little ones and braced ourselves as we sent out the call that dinner was ready: What a picture to remember with all of us seated at the table laden with food; Gerri led Grace, and our only comment during the meal was, "God love their appetites."

After dinner, the older children were off again to roam around the farm. On holidays such as this, we usually dispensed the older boys from their dishwashing chores; one of the girls usually helped us out, but Dolores and I had more time to talk as we cleaned up.

Just as she and I finished the cleanup and sat down with another cup of coffee, the door opened and the outside adventurers filed in with a chorus of voices. "We're hungry, what have you got to eat?"

Dolores and I looked at each other and said, "God love their appetites."

The Monday after Thanksgiving brought typical Michigan weather—extremely cold. Terry was scheduled to take our bus, the Troubadour, to Chicago for use in the project; however, this morning, he couldn't convince the engine to start. After all, it had never been asked to start in the winter before; we always took our trips in it in the summer.

While working on this, he received a phone call from John. He came into the kitchen looking very concerned.

"A car struck Wilbur as he walked across an intersection in his hometown of LaPorte, Indiana: He's in the hospital there."

"Is it life threatening?"

"John said his leg is broken, but he'll be all right. I'll stop at LaPorte and see him."

I could see that Terry was quite concerned about this development and what effect it would have on the project.

With some tender loving care to the engine, the Troubadour left with only Terry on board. I followed him through town to the highway. Tears came to my eyes as I saw it go down the highway; all the other times the whole family was on board. The time would come though, when we'd be together again.

The first week in December, Terry called.

"I'd like you to meet me in LaPorte: John, Rose, Tom, and I are going to visit Wilbur in the hospital."

"There's no forecast of snow for the next few days. I should make it without weather problems."

I took down the directions and made plans to go to Indiana.

Sunday morning, having left Terry, Jr., in charge of the family, I started off for La Porte. I didn't encounter any weather problems until I reached the bottom of Lake Michigan: That spot received the lake-effect snow. I could hardly see through the wind-driven snow. As I neared La Porte though, the skies cleared again.

John, Rose, Tom, Terry, and I, along with Rosario, Fernando, and Ana Maria had lunch together before going to the hospital; I really enjoyed seeing all of them again. During the lunch, our conversation turned to packing for Peru. I had many questions to ask Rosario: what type of clothing should we bring, what schools were available, would we need home schooling provisions? We also talked about useful Christmas gifts to buy. By the end of the lunch, I had pages of notes; it had been a real working lunch for us.

During visiting hours at the hospital, we took turns going up to see Wilbur. His right leg was badly injured, but he seemed in good spirits and was taking it all very well. As we left the hospital, I said goodbye to the Peruvian family. I would not have the opportunity of seeing them again.

Late that afternoon, Terry and I drove back to Grand Haven; the countryside was aglow with the sunlight on the freshly fallen snow. The air was cold and crisp. We had a chance to do lots of talking, and we thoroughly enjoyed the trip home.

All the children were so happy to see us when we arrived; they engulfed Dad for a while. They stayed up past their 8:00 o'clock bedtime so everyone could get a chance to tell Dad all their news. We finally convinced them that they would never get up in time for school if they didn't get off to bed, so up the stairs they went. Terry left the next afternoon on the train.

About the middle of December, the instructors went to take a course at Allison Transmission School (General Motors, Inc.) in Indianapolis, Indiana as part of their training. The school offered them the week-long course as their contribution to the project. The instructors planned to take the bus to live in while at the school; they also made plans to stop off in La Porte to visit Wilbur on their way to Indianapolis.

Terry called Friday to inform me of their plans.

"I'd like you and the kids to come to La Porte Sunday. We're stopping there to visit Wilbur on our way to Indianapolis; that will give the kids a chance to see us and Wilbur."

"We'll be there. The children will be delighted to see all of you."

Sunday, with my 16-quart Presto full of chili, and loaves of home-made bread to go with it, we started out for La Porte. We found our way to the hospital and there stood the Troubadour in the parking lot waiting for us: We had a grand reunion with the instructors during our lunch in the bus.

However, when we went into the hospital, they informed us that Wilbur had experienced complications during the night: He was quite ill with a staph infection. We took turns peeking in to say *hello* so we wouldn't tire him too much.

After visiting hours we said good-bye to Dad and all the men. We watched the bus take off down the highway on their way to Indianapolis. Then we turned north and followed the shore of Lake Michigan to Grand Haven.

Christmas Eve came, and with the children in bed, Terry and I sat looking at the tree which sparkled with its trimmings: this was our special time before putting all the gifts under the tree. We looked at the shepherds standing with their sheep by the pool of water and some other shepherds in the stable nearby. Mary and Joseph rested by the cow and the donkey: all awaiting the coming of Baby Jesus.

Each Christmas was like this. The children loved to help me set up the crib: The moss on the hillside served for grass; we gathered the moss, along with small stones for the pathways, from the backyard in early

December before the deep snows set in; brown paper bags served as the hills and a small piece of blue glass for the pool of water. The children found this glass by the Church when a storm broke the glass from windows in the church tower. When all was in place, they checked over everything before going to bed to see that all was in order.

Christmas morning, after Mass, the children lined up by the living room door, ready to go and see if Baby Jesus came during the night: There He lay in the manger, with the angel hovering over the entrance of the stable and the shepherds, sheep and dog looking in. Then over to the tree they went to unwrap the presents Santa left.

Aunt Fanny, Terry's mother's sister, came for Christmas dinner; she had lived alone since Uncle Tom died: She enjoyed the dinner and all the festivities.

"I haven't talked so much for a long time; it's so nice to be with all of you."

As we settled back after dinner, Terry said, "Let's call Grandma McCarthy and wish her a Merry Christmas. Then Aunt Fanny can talk to her sister, too."

"We want to talk to Grandma, too," came a chorus of voices of the children.

So Grandma McCarthy joined in our Christmas celebration.

By mid-afternoon though, Aunt Fanny grew tired; she was not accustomed to such a lively bunch around. She and Uncle Tom hadn't had any children.

"Thank you so much for inviting me to dinner today; it's been such a lovely day, but I think it's time for me to go home."

"It's been such a pleasure to have you with us," I said, giving her a big hug, and soon she was engulfed with hugs from all the children.

In the evening, with all the toy trucks and equipment parked back under the tree, the doll sleeping alongside Brigid, Terry and I enjoyed looking over it all before going to bed.

The next day Terry's sister, Ginny, and her family came to visit us. We warned her ahead of time that we intended to farm out some of our prized possessions in preparation for our move. She became the lucky custodian of all of our record albums: They were near and dear to us and gave us many hours of enjoyment. Most of them were 78s, some Terry's, others I received when I worked for Rush Hughes, a disc jockey on KXOK in St. Louis and some from Capitol Records when I worked there. Another large portion of the classical records came from a photographer, Frank Nouss: I worked for him after school during my high school years.

I visited Frank on one of my trips to see my family in Missouri. Frank had purchased all his favorite classical music on long-play, 33 1/3 records.

"Would you like to have the 78s?"

This is like asking me if I like ice cream. "Yes, yes—I would love to have them: thanks for the offer, Frank."

Getting them back to Michigan, though, presented a problem: I had come to Missouri on the train. Frank's wife, Tillie, suggested we pack them in a couple of their suitcases, then I could send the suitcases back. That sounded like a good idea, so that's what we did.

The weight of a suitcase filled with 78 rpm records is something to be reckoned with; my brother carried them to the door of the train for me; he could hardly manage them. The porter came walking toward us.

"I'll take them aboard."

His first try didn't even budge them from the ground: Then he really got serious about it and carried them aboard; after he stowed them away, he gave me a hard look.

"Lady, I've picked up some heavy suitcases in my day, but these have got to be the heaviest—what in the world do you have in them?"

I was almost afraid to tell him. "Just some 78 rpm records."

"You'd better tell the next person who tries to carry them, what's in them before *they* try to pick them up."

I put loaves of home-made bread into the suitcases when I sent them back; Frank and Tillie were delighted.

We had also asked Terry's sister, Ginny, to keep a big platter and covered dish we received from Aunt Kate, another of Grandma McCarthy's sisters. It was English china and very beautiful.

I had seen them in her pantry one day when I visited her.

"Aunt Kate, what a lovely set that is."

"That was a wedding gift from my mother-in-law, but I hardly ever use them."

One day she came to visit us, and in her hands was the platter and covered dish.

"I want you to have them, but you must promise me that you'll use them *now* while all your children are young; I never did that, and I have always regretted it."

"I will promise to do that, Aunt Kate."

I kept my promise and have always used them.

The following day our family left for Chicago to spend a few days of the Christmas vacation with John and his family and the other instructors. We stayed in the apartment where the Peruvian family had lived. The six-month training period ended, so they moved out. The Third Order Fraternity of Arlington Heights furnished the apartment originally with articles they collected; now some things were kept for the project for the move to Texas, and the rest went to families in the area.

During my visit John made arrangements for his wife, Rose, and I to meet with a doctor from Peru doing some research at the Children's Hospital in Chicago: We hoped to get some helpful information from him regarding the health problems we might face with the children of all ages in our group, from teens to very young ones. It turned out to be a very interesting day.

Several other doctors came in to join in the discussion; one had recently returned from the hospital ship HOPE, anchored off the coast of Ecuador. We discussed what precautions to take with the children and what we could expect along the lines of diseases. They all agreed amoebas presented one of the major problems: We would need to boil water, not only for drinking, but also for brushing teeth.

The doctor from the hospital ship said we'd have a problem of local mothers bringing their children to us.

"When they see your healthy children, they will want their children to look the same; they'll want to give you their children so they'll get better food and health care."

That threw me a curve, and I wondered how I would deal with that.

I was quite pregnant with Camille at the time, and the doctor from Peru said: "I hope you intend to breast feed the new baby; that will eliminate a lot of problems.

"I do intend to breast feed the new baby, Doctor: I always breast feed my babies."

It was a very informative day and we were grateful for the time the doctors spent with us.

The following day one of my brothers, Harold, a bank examiner in the Chicago area whom I hadn't seen in quite a few years, came to dinner. He had met Terry, Jr., Kevin, Rory, and Bob one time on a visit to Grand Haven; now he met the rest of the family, Cronan, Sean, Christopher, Brigid, and Hilary. We had a very enjoyable evening.

The last day at the apartment turned a little hectic. Terry, Terry, Jr., Kevin, and Rory went with John on some errands. While the rest of the children and I finished up the last bit of packing, Brigid locked herself in the upstairs bathroom. She was two and a half years old then; I worried about what she might get into before we could get her out. We looked everywhere for the instrument to unlock the door from outside, but couldn't find it; we looked for a ladder to get into the bathroom window; no one in the neighborhood had one. I called the Real Estate Company, but after many calls, no one came to help us. In the meantime, Christopher lay on the floor in front of the door to keep Brigid's attention down there: Hopefully that would keep her out of other things in the bathroom. I talked to her quite a long time, too.

"Brigid, you're a big girl and I know you can push the latch and open the door."

I kept trying to convince her to open the door from the inside, but to no avail.

Instead she said, "Look what I found, Mommy," and shoved a razor blade under the door. I was so frightened!

The children diverted her attention by playing a game of passing paper under the door while I went to call the fire department.

"Mom, she's not shoving the paper back to us anymore."

Just then the doorbell rang: I opened the door and the man from the telephone company stood there.

"Hello, Madam, I'm here to disconnect the phone."

I welcomed him with open arms. He looked a little startled at the greeting.

"Come upstairs, please, and unlock the bathroom door."

He followed me as I ran up the stairs and when he reached the door, cautioned me.

"You didn't see me do this."

With one of his tools, he pried the door jam and unlocked the door. As it flew open, Brigid lay sound asleep on the floor. Our hero celebrated along with us as I gathered her into my arms.

New Year's Day, we went to Mass in Arlington Heights, said goodbye to everyone, and then went back to Grand Haven. The New Year started off with one of the instructors, Tom Putzbach, leaving the project: Now we had two instructors, Wilbur and Terry, and the director, John. January, with its cold and snowy weather, set in with some difficult decisions to make.

The donated equipment was available for the move to Texas, where it would be readied for shipment to Peru: a scraper, a dozer, a front-end loader, and the training materials and manuals for them from Clark Equipment Company of Benton Harbor, Michigan, plus slides and manuals from Allison Division, GMC in Indianapolis for their equipment's torquematic transmissions. However, we had no word from the Board of the Vico Nechhi Apostolate on their commitment to provide funds. John was reaching the end of his resources.

We decided to continue on. We purchased a lowboy and an old GMC tractor from a man in Grand Haven to haul the equipment to Texas. The lowboy needed a little work done on it. The tractor,

10 AMBASSADORS TO COSTA RICA

however, left a lot to be desired; it was an old army 6 x 6 with only a piece of canvas as the covering for the cab. It did not include a heater in the list of extras.

Dressed like Eskimos, John and Terry left Grand Haven in zero degree weather, one in the tractor with the lowboy, the other in a car. They planned to swap off driving the tractor and the car on their way to Benton Harbor, Michigan to pick up training materials from Clark Equipment Company, and then on to Arlington Heights. We all hoped the cold would be tolerable.

Rose called me when the frozen twosome reached Arlington Heights, long overdue: What happened in between, only John and Terry knew for sure, and we could only imagine.

I had mixed emotions when Terry went off to Texas from Arlington Heights with the first load on the bus: The bus did have a heater. We kept in touch by phone. He had been so terribly cold for so long, and now he daily told me how he shed his coat, his jacket, and now felt fine with just his sweatshirt. I was glad he was getting warm, but he also was getting farther and farther away.

As we awaited the birth of our eleventh child, I debated whether to take the doctor's advice to induce labor *before* my due date: In the past, we waited until after. He assured me the baby wouldn't come if it was not ready. I decided to go ahead with the procedure on February 4.

Terry returned to Grand Haven on the train. I entered the hospital in the morning and the inductions began intravenously in the afternoon. The doctor spent his "afternoon off" with me while he monitored the procedure. All went well, and as they prepared to wheel me into the delivery room, the doctor asked me, "Should I call Terry, or should we let him feed the children first?"

"He can't be in the delivery room anyway, so let's let him feed the children first."

So Camille came into the world: She was a beautiful baby, just like the rest of our babies. But I couldn't believe she had red hair. Terry's

49

uncle George had red hair and green eyes, but Terry's Dad had black hair and very blue eyes, as did Terry. Now we had one daughter, Brigid, with black hair and blue eyes and another daughter, Camille, with red hair and green eyes: We were so happy about that.

Later, the doctor came into our room.

"You don't owe me anything for this delivery. I know you don't have insurance coverage right now so that's my contribution to your project."

"Thank you, Doctor; we really appreciate everything that you've done for us."

Terry stayed with us until I was back on the job, and then he returned to Texas.

PROMISES

Cold

silent

winter,

unrelenting strength;

at each turn

growing stronger.

Should we give in

or press on?

We'll go on

for each passing day

brings closer

the promise

of spring.

Chapter III

Preparation and Move to Texas

Terry, Jr., Kevin, Rory, Bob, and Cronan spent all the time not devoted to doing lessons, on sorting and packing our belongings. We tried to stick to packing only the necessary things and gave away many things we couldn't take along. At times, the packing seemed an insurmountable task, but we just kept packing.

I ran into more difficulty with Camille than we expected. She slept too much, and therefore, was not eating enough. I set the alarm every two hours to feed her. Then I worked on waking her up and getting her to eat. I tried every kind of trick to keep her awake while breast feeding; that proved almost impossible. Consequently, her demand did not keep the milk flowing very well: She gained weight very slowly. We went to see the doctor.

"You'll have to supplement her with milk from the bottle: Cut the hole in the nipple bigger to force her to swallow when the milk comes out."

"I'll try that, doctor. I hope it works."

That process did help but it proved quite difficult and very time-consuming. Needless to say, I spent most of my time with Camille.

I received many phone calls during that time from friends and neighbors; they told me how sorry they felt for me, and that they would try to get over and help. When some did come, I walked around them as they sat and told me that I was taking the brunt of the work of the project. I was here by myself: The rest of the people in the project got off easy. After a few of those visits, when someone called that wanted to help, I told them in a nice way that we were doing fine and really didn't need any help.

But I enjoyed the visits from Joan McCarthy, Terry's cousin's wife. We were very good friends and spent a lot of time together. Julia and Mickey McReynolds's visits were treasures too; Mickey was the Prefect of the Third Order Fraternity in Muskegon, the Fraternity to which Terry and I belonged. They always brought something sweet for the kids and lots of cheer and help for us.

One luxury we didn't give up was the weekly phone call from Terry on Sunday night: We could hardly wait for the phone to ring. He called collect because he was always on the move. One month we didn't have the money to pay for the phone bill: Funds in the project were low and we couldn't pay it just then. I talked with the lady at the phone company.

"We cannot pay the bill right now, but it will be paid before we leave; we can't get along without our weekly call. It's our lifeline."

"I'll take care of the bill for you. You can come to the office and see me when you have the money."

She took care of the bill with her own money: What a complete stranger did for me that day, I will never forget. I went to her office to pay the bill and thank her before we left. Terry's sister, Ginny, called us every week, too: she was a very special person.

Sunday afternoons the children and I went visiting to say goodbye to our special friends and relatives. We also wanted to make one last visit to the grave of our little son, Joe, who died in 1948 when he was just a few hours old. I'll never forget the Sunday when we decided to do that. We first visited Mrs. LaPenna, a sweet Italian lady; we often picked her up when we saw her walking home after Mass. She loved the children and was so sad that we were leaving.

As we left her house she said, "I'm so afraid one of the children will be left behind somewhere at an airport."

"You don't have to worry about that. I always take care to check that everyone is accounted for."

I had to eat my words that day.

We drove across town to the cemetery. As we prepared to leave the car, I gasped: Hilary, our youngest son was not with us. I remembered seeing one of the older boys getting him dressed to go outside and then saw him outside on the walk: I knew he went outside. That trip across town to Mrs. LaPenna's house was the longest trip I ever made!

She was waiting for us to come back: The look on her face told it all. I took Hilary in my arms and hugged him tightly.

"This will never happen again, I promise you."

"After you left, I heard some whimpering outside the house. I went out and there was Hilary standing on the walkway around the other side of the house: That's why you didn't see him."

"I've learned my lesson, believe me. We'll call each child by name before we move on. The little one assigned to one of the older boys will have them in sight at all times."

We finally heard from the Vico Nechi Apostolate. They informed John that they no longer had interest in the project; they felt the donated equipment, titled to ITAF, would expose them to liability. They had organized for the purpose of developing financial support and to aid in recruiting personnel. To date, we had received no financial or recruiting services from them. It was a loss, but not a great loss.

Needless to say, one doesn't stop living, and being this far along, we decided to go on with the move. It would be necessary to find work in Texas and continue on with plans to go to Peru with different backing.

Meanwhile, back in Grand Haven, Terry's cousin, Chuck, and his wife, Joan, invited me to their home for coffee. This turned out to be a big surprise farewell party for me: They surely did surprise me. Many neighbors and friends were there. they gave me a Benrus watch as a remembrance from all of them. It was a wonderful evening.

A few days later, a man knocked at the door and presented his police badge: a plainclothesman from the State Police. *Has something happened to Terry?*

"May I come in?"

"Yes, of course." I trembled wondering what he would tell me.

"May I see all the children, please?"

"Terry, Kevin, Rory, Bob, and Cronan are in school; here are Sean, Christopher, Brigid, Hilary, and Camille."

"Well they all look fine and healthy to me. Someone reported that you have no visible means of support since your husband is living in Texas: They felt you were guilty of child neglect."

We have been pulled through some knot-holes in our lifetime, but I don't think any of them hurt as much as this one did. He would not, of course, tell me who reported it. He said the person told him they drove by the house almost every day and couldn't stand thinking that the children might be suffering with nothing being done about it.

"If they know us and drive by, why didn't they stop and talk to us?" I asked with tears streaming down my face, "I think that might have been a more humane way to do it."

"I guess many have grown to feel that an agency can take care of all the helping out that is needed."

"I can't imagine how anyone who knows us could think we were guilty of child abuse."

I had quite an extended conversation with the policeman. He was a fine gentleman. I explained to him what we wanted to accomplish and why we wanted to do it; he said he thought it was something that should be pursued.

As he was leaving, he said, "I wish all families were as well taken care of as your family. Please call me anytime if you would just like to talk."

"Thank you. I've never felt as rich as I do right now: I feel sorry for the poverty of the person who reported us."

I did call him and just talked several times after that.

In April, Terry came home on the train. The next couple of days he spent driving our car back and forth to Arlington Heights with loads to be put on the lowboy in preparation for the move to Texas. With the last-minute packing completed, the Checker bulged at the seams: It made the trip to Wisconsin look quite small in comparison. We took a last look at our house and were on our way to Michigan City, Indiana.

There Terry and two of our sons, Rory and Kevin, switched over to the White tractor which John had purchased and left there; their next stop was Arlington Heights. There the lowboy, loaded with training materials for the heavy equipment, and also with canned food the Fraternity in Arlington Heights gathered for us, was attached to the White tractor; Terry and the boys continued their journey to my folks in Missouri. I drove the rest of the family in our car. We arrived just a little ahead of Terry.

Mom and Dad hosted quite a reunion for our farewell party. All my sisters and brothers and their families came: Marcella, Marian, Jerome, Georgia, Harold, Richard, Rosemary, Joan, Beatrice, and Carol and Terry's youngest brother, Gene, and his wife, Barb. It was quite a sendoff! I can only imagine how Mom and Dad felt as they saw us take off with all our possessions for parts unknown.

We then proceeded on by car and truck to Everman, Texas. The trip from Michigan to Texas was a very pleasant one; in Grand Haven, we left melting snow and cold weather; spring burst forth with tulips and hyacinths blooming in Missouri. Mom's garden was such a delight to see. Beds of yellow roses greeted us at the motel in Texas: We have fond memories of that trip.

John chose Everman, Texas as the staging area. A contractor offered him the use of a large building on land he owned, an old Army air base: The contractor was subdividing the land. One part of the building housed the dozer and front end loader; another part served as living quarters for John's family and Wilbur. The contractor used our dozer in subdividing the land.

When we arrived at the staging area, the Troubadour stood alongside the building: what a welcome sight! We had our house on wheels; it was our home again even though only on a temporary basis.

·

REALITY

Cold

silent

winter's

waning strength

released

the warmth

of spring.

Melting snow

turned into

beds of tulips

then to roses

as we

journeyed south

Chapter IV

Campsite in Texas

Our stay in Everman, Texas was short. John met Frank Yaeger, a member of the Third Order Fraternity in Fort Worth. He talked to him about the project; Frank showed interest in it and wanted to take part in it.

"Where's your camp set up now?"

"We're just outside Everman in an equipment storage building."

"I'm part owner of a ranch near Lake Benbrook; I have a spot there perfect for your campsite; you're welcome to use it. There's a possibility of doing some work for me, too."

John went to the ranch to check it out and decided to take his offer. The site, on a hillside, offered a very pleasant view of the bottomland on an arm of the Trinity River; nearby, stood a little cabin in a grove of live oak trees alongside a windmill by a millpond. This assured a supply of nice, fresh water for us. A black man, known to us only as Curtis, lived with his wife in the little cabin. He worked for Frank on the ranch.

Our little city consisted of two large tents, an office tent with a large screened-in section, two small tents, and our bus, the Troubadour. John Murphy's family: his wife, Rose, and daughters, Ann, Patricia, and Kate, and a son, Terry, occupied one large tent. Their son, Mike lived in a small tent alongside it. Wilbur used the closed-in section of the office tent for his sleeping room. Our family lived in the bus and the other large tent. Another small tent served as a store room.

While we were in the process of getting settled into our little city, it started to rain and it kept on raining; at that time I didn't know Texas got that much rain. We finally left the cars near the highway because they couldn't navigate the mud down the long lane to our site; we used the Jeep as the shuttle between camp and the highway. Down in the bottomland, we could see the Trinity River, spilling over its banks now, and flowing into Lake Benbrook.

During this time, I made arrangements at a Spanish church in Fort Worth for Cronan to make his First Holy Communion. We brought along the documents from our parish in Michigan indicating that he started preparation there. He joined a class in Fort Worth preparing for their First Communion.

On the Sunday morning for the celebration, the rain continued falling. Terry looked around outside the bus and then returned.

"I think just you and Cronan will go this morning. It's just too hard to get everyone out to the highway."

"I guess there's nothing else we can do. We'll celebrate with everyone when we come back."

Terry carried Cronan through the mud to the Jeep. I followed wearing some old shoes and carrying my other shoes with me: Cronan and I made it to the Church. He received Our Lord for the first time during the Mass. Father celebrated the Mass in the Spanish language with a few more rituals than we were accustomed to. The white dresses and veils looked beautiful on the little, dark-eyed girls. The families of the children graciously invited Cronan and me for breakfast after Mass in the Church Hall. It was a grand celebration.

At home, everyone gathered in the bus for brunch; the cake I baked for the occasion looked pretty good despite the fact that someone had sat on it in the crowded conditions of the bus.

The weather finally settled down, and the life at camp reached a routine. Between the two large tents, under some mesquite trees, the men built a wooden wash stand for the children; a bench on one side helped Chris, Brigid and Hilary reach the counter top. Their names painted above their places set it off nicely. Each morning they got a bowl of water to wash their faces and a cup of water to brush their teeth; a drain behind the counter top handled the water they poured out as they finished.

Near the wash stand, the men built a shower stall with a rack above the stall. Terry used the front-end loader to transport a 50-gallon drum to the millpond; there he filled the drum with water and then brought it back up the hill and placed it on the rack above the shower stall. The children loved to watch Dad get the water and put the drum in place with the loader. The sun heated the water in the drum to a perfect temperature for a shower. This was the first solar power we ever used.

Nature kept providing us with new and exciting things. The sunsets were in a class all by themselves; bright orange rays reached high up into the sky and bathed everything around us in its glow: All ceased to move for those few minutes as the magic caught us and held us. At night, with no electric lights to give them competition, the stars looked so much larger and brighter. We rolled up the sides of the tent to let in the cooling breezes; on a moonlit night, we could see many of the nocturnal animals running about. It was a real study in nature for the children.

It took quite a while for me to get accustomed to the vastness of the countryside; it made me wonder how the pioneers felt as they traveled through. On one of our trips to Lake Benbrook, Cronan saw a historic marker along the road.

"Mom, let's go see what's on that marker."

"Okay, let's have a look."

"Gosh, Mom, that's part of the Chisholm Trail."

"I've heard about that trail many times; now I know where part of it is."

"The plaque says it was the major route out of Texas for livestock. Scot-Cherokee Jesse Chisholm made the first tracks; he began hauling trade goods to Indian camps in 1864."

"I see they used it only from 1867 to 1884 for moving cattle; it sure covered a lot of territory though, from the Rio Grande to central Kansas. Well, we learned some history today, didn't we."

Back at camp, all the men went out daily to look for work. John went to work for an advertising firm in Fort Worth; his salary made up our cash flow at that time.

One evening when he arrived back at camp, he walked over to us with a big smile on his face.

"At the office today, I found it a little difficult to concentrate on ways to advertise some mink-lined golf club covers."

That was the quote of the day!

The big load of canned goods we brought from Arlington Heights complemented our diet. When haying time came, Frank contracted Terry, Terry, Jr., and Kevin to cut and bring in hay for him. He also hired Rory and Bob to hoe the corn planted nearby. That job gave Rory some trouble though. The cornfield was near Curtis's cabin; the dog belonging to Curtis took a disliking to Rory. The bite marks on Rory's leg proved it. When Rory saw the dog coming, he ran and climbed anything available to get out of his way. Bob, never afraid of anything, found that hilarious, much to Rory's chagrin. Needless to say, Rory did not have pleasant memories of that job.

As the haying job finished, Frank met with John.

"My brother and I are developing a housing project called 'Mustang Meadows' on another part of the ranch. We need a road cut there, and I think you can handle the job with your dozer."

"Terry and I can take a look at it; be with you in a minute."

John and Terry went with Frank and accepted the job offer. John surveyed and set the stakes for the road; Terry brought the dozer over and cut the road: Frank and his brother were very pleased with the work. After a hot, dusty day of working, Lake Benbrook always looked very inviting.

During the hot weather, bread baking presented some problems. No matter where we went, I always started baking bread as soon as possible because when the children smelled bread baking, it was home again. But here, in the hot dry air, I looked for cooler, damper places to let it raise; in Michigan, I had looked for a warm place to put it.

John's daughter, Patricia, came to the bus one day when she smelled the bread baking.

"Would you teach me how to bake bread? It smells so good."

"Of course I will. Here, have a piece that I just buttered."

"This is so good. Let me know when you're going to bake again and I'll be here."

A few days later, we made bread together.

"Kneading the dough is hard work. How many loaves does this make?"

"I always make six one-pound loaves, so it is a big batch."

"I didn't know the dough raises twice before you can make it into loaves: This is a long process."

"Yes, I know; then we have to wait until it raises in the pans before we can bake them. You'll be here for quite a while."

When the bread came out of the oven and was cooling, one proud girl triumphantly raced across to her tent with the loaves of bread. I blessed the day we bought that stove for our bus. It turned out bread or a birthday cake almost on a daily basis.

Even though Peru still worked on making final arrangements for our move there, the schedule for it was long overdue. John told them he was forced to make contacts to go to other countries.

The Rural Development Officer of the AID Mission in Costa Rica, Carl Koone, came to the States to look for some way to train operators and mechanics to build and repair roads on the Nicoyan Peninsula of Costa Rica. When he heard about our project, he contacted John and made arrangements with him to come and visit our camp site.

John escorted Carl around the camp; he looked at the equipment and talked with the members of the families. He came to the door of the bus.

"Do I smell bread baking? I can hardly believe you bake your own bread out here."

"Yes, I do bake bread—would you like a piece from the loaf that's cooled?"

"I certainly would."

After he finished eating the bread, he walked over to the playpen and played with Camille's fingers.

"You sure look like you're doing well in these conditions, little girl. Mrs. McCarthy, I talked with your other children too: I don't think any of you will have problems living with the people on the Peninsula in Costa Rica."

"We'd sure like to try, Mr. Koone."

Ultimately, Carl thought that our group could do the job he had in mind. He asked John to go to Costa Rica with him to assess the work there. John went with him and felt satisfied that we could handle the work. He subsequently signed a two-year contract for ITAF to go to Costa Rica.

Now we started to inventory and pack all our belongings for shipping. We also scheduled appointments for complete physical examinations along with the whole series of shots necessary for traveling overseas. Another requisite was passport pictures; my passport picture included all ten of the children with me: They didn't make individual passports for the children at that time. I still have that passport with all the health books of the shots we received for the children and me. It is quite a package. All of this meant lots of showers and many trips with the front end loader down to the mill pond for water.

The typhoid shots left some of the children sick. Bob and Cronan were the most serious. Our tent turned into a hospital of sorts. During that time, in the summer's heat, we welcomed the sound of the windmill beginning to turn; that meant nice, cool, fresh water on a hot afternoon for our patients.

During this time, Terry brought the GMC tractor from Arlington Heights. He went there by plane and then drove down in the tractor. I remembered that first trip he took in the tractor with the canvas cab in sub-zero weather in Michigan; now he made the trip in the intense heat of the Southwest, another chapter in the saga of the GMC.

Wilbur continued to have complications with his broken leg and decided to leave the project. Now, John added the job of finding another instructor to replace him to his roster. He moved his office to the Rodeway Inn in Fort Worth to simplify the work.

On the 6th of July, Terry, the children, and I enjoyed a little picnic by Lake Benbrook. We celebrated our first anniversary with ITAF. Dad surprised us all with a display of fireworks. He bought them on his way down from Arlington Heights. It was a fitting way to start our second year with ITAF. A year before we celebrated with the Men's Choir in Grand Haven as we said our good-byes to all of them; now we celebrated our departure from Texas and started our journey to new places.

Before Wilbur left he made small wooden boxes for each of the children, and most of the clothes were packed into them. By the middle of July, the first load was on its way to Houston for crating and shipping. We slowly broke up camp. We were actually on our way. What would the next two years bring? That was a very fascinating thought!

Texas Camp

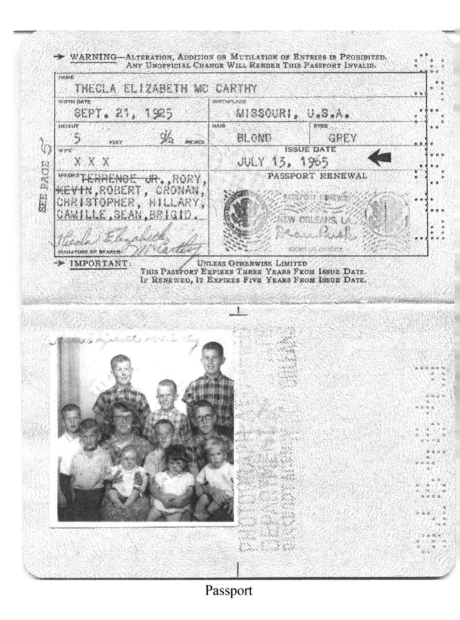

NAME
THECLA ELIZABETH MC CARTHY

BIRTH DATE
SEPT. 21, 1925

BIRTHPLACE
MISSOURI, U.S.A.

HEIGHT
5 FEET 9½ INCHES

HAIR
BLOND

EYES
GREY

WIFE
X X X

ISSUE DATE
JULY 13, 1965

MINORS
TERRENCE JR., RORY, KEVIN, ROBERT, CRONAN, CHRISTOPHER, HILLARY, CAMILLE, SEAN, BRIGID.

PASSPORT RENEWAL

SIGNATURE OF BEARER

SEE PAGE 5

Passport

Chapter V

On Our Way

Dusk settled in at the campsite. It was time to call it a day. We stopped our packing and cleaning and went to the Rodeway Inn, our home until our departure for Houston. We were sunburned and dusty; the coolness of the motel felt heavenly. It felt odd, though, to have carpeting and air conditioning after living in tents for two and a half months. Refreshed by the shower we enjoyed our dinner; then the beds looked very inviting. The air conditioning, however, proved to be too much and we turned it off for the night.

Each day we returned to campsite to continue our job of cleaning up and stacking lumber, putting things we would not take along into the bus. Frank gave us permission to leave the Troubadour parked in the grove of live oak trees near the windmill. That would be a pleasant place for it to stay. Each evening we stopped off in the town of Benbrook to do the laundry; each day also, another load of things went to Houston for crating and shipping.

Thursday, July 22, 1965, John signed a contract with another Instructor, Ed Clark, to fill the spot vacated by Wilbur. Ed's wife, Martha and two daughters, Laura and Catherine, would also join us.

Saturday they loaded the dozer for Houston. It was the last load for a common carrier. Terry and the Clark family received their yellow-fever shots that day. Sunday, after Mass, we checked out of the Rodeway Inn and met back at campsite where the loaded lowboy waited. From there we proceeded by jeep, station wagon, and our car to Houston. Terry followed with the GMC and lowboy, yet another chapter in the life of Terry and the GMC.

He arrived at Gulf Port Crating in Houston on Monday at noon. All the project equipment was loaded on the *SS Managua* of the Mamenic Lines, flying the Nicaraguan flag, their destination: Puntarenas, Costa Rica. A waiver allowed us to ship on other than a U.S. ship.

In Houston, we lived in the Helena Motel. With only the laundry to do at the Laundromat, I just sat and relaxed for a while. Tuesday the new family arrived by plane. I think they set a record for completing moving arrangements: In just six days, they had stored all their things they wanted to keep, sold what needed selling, packed, gotten passports, gotten shots, and moved to Houston.

John purchased the airline tickets and obtained the visas. Saturday they took the luggage to the airport and checked it through to San Jose. The jeep and station wagon shipped out with the other equipment; we kept the car until Saturday evening and then parted company with our Checker on a used car lot: we had a kind of sad parting.

Sunday morning, August 1, 1965, we checked out of the Helena Motel; the limousines picked us up at 6:00. The next stop was the airport.

Because of the preparations made the day before, in a matter of 10 to 15 minutes, we checked through the Pan Am ticket counter. Our group loaded first, seventeen children and six adults in all. A bassinet mounted on the front bulkhead of the plane served as the seat for Camille. We enjoyed the trip very much. It was the first jet flight for the children and me.

In Mexico City, I bought a nice, leather passport container. It was large enough for the passport and eleven health books as well. A few minutes later, we took off for Guatemala. After a brief stop there, we continued on to San Jose.

We landed at Coco International Airport about one o'clock in the afternoon. We couldn't help but think of those twenty-three duffel bags, plus a few suitcases and carry-on bags going through Customs. Would it take a long time? Would they open it all up and go through it all?

We lined them up on the ramp; the man looked at them and at John.

"This is all in one group, right?"

"Yes sir, it is."

Here, I think, we set a record on getting through Customs; perhaps they considered seventeen children a little too many to contain for any length of time.

Neil Fine, who represented the AID Mission in San Jose, welcomed us. Quite a few cars and station wagons lined up to transport us into San Jose; this ride provided some spine-tingling moments. The driver hardly ever looked ahead; he kept a lively conversation going with his face turned toward us as he managed to skirt around and through all sorts of traffic, horn honking through the near misses. (At first I thought that I would never want to drive here but later regretted that I didn't have the opportunity. It fascinated me, and on several occasions, I felt the urge to ask the cab driver to let me try.)

We arrived at the Holland House Hotel, a beautiful hotel situated on a hill just outside of San Jose. The brilliant sun bathed the countryside, and a warm soft breeze brought the scent of flowers with it. Mr. Fine checked us into the hotel. After getting settled in, we went to the dining room where Carl Koone and Percy Shaw, Executive Officer of USAID welcomed us.

At the church where we went to Mass in the evening, we encountered volcanic ash piled up in the corner by the steps of the church, evidence of the recent eruption of Mount Irazu. Even though the Mass was offered in the Spanish language, the Sacrifice remains the same everywhere in the world. We returned to the hotel in heavy rain—we learned right off that the weather changed quickly here.

The next morning, first things first, I looked for the laundry to wash diapers. The ladies working there became our very good friends. They thought it a little strange, though, that I washed my own clothes.

In the dining room, a large table was reserved for our family. Served formally, the dinners were very pleasant. On our son, Kevin's birthday, I met with the owner's wife.

"Would you order a cake for Kevin's birthday and serve it with dinner this evening?"

"Yes, of course I will."

After dinner that evening, the lights dimmed, a beautifully decorated cake with thirteen candles on it rolled out of the kitchen on a little cart; a young man with an accordion accompanied it. So, with all the diners joining in, we sang *Happy Birthday* to Kevin and enjoyed his very unique thirteenth birthday party. It was a pleasant surprise for all of us.

One day, while we were seated at the table for lunch, everything began to rattle. The vase of flowers on the table began to sway slightly back and forth. The floor began to sway ever so slightly; it felt like a swinging bridge. People started running out of the dining room; we stayed at our table, and the swaying stopped just as suddenly as it started. We continued on with our lunch; this was our first encounter with an earthquake.

I experienced some pangs of homesickness those first few days. The tropical blue-green color of the vegetation and the frequent heavy showers presented quite a change. But as I walked around on the roads by the hotel, I found that life is truly the same everywhere. I heard a baby cry and the sound of the mother comforting the baby; I heard the happy sound of children playing; I received friendly greetings as I met people. All of these things are the same everywhere; the language is different, but the feelings are the same.

During our short stay in San Jose, we had dinner with Carl Koone and his family at their home. At another time, Mrs. Al Farwell, the Mission Director's wife, received the ladies of our group at a morning coffee. During that visit she received a phone call.

She looked at us.

"The Ambassador wishes to receive you, your husbands, and the children this afternoon at his office."

We apologized to Mrs. Farwell for our abrupt departure and rushed across town to the hotel to bathe and dress the children.

Terry, Ed, and John, at different places in the city on separate assignments, received the message of the meeting with the Ambassador. As Rose, Martha, I, and our children arrived in the parking lot of the Embassy, John, Ed, and Terry arrived also—all in separate vehicles.

We all looked at each other, and John made the comment.

"Are we good or what!"

We all walked into the Ambassador's office right on time.

Now it was time to say goodbye to the Holland House and start journeying across the mountains to Puntarenas. We always remembered the warmth of the people at the Holland House. Their graciousness to us as strangers in a foreign country meant so much. It was time now to go on to another stopover.

NIC

Sea-level coastal plain
Caribbean shores, and r
with towering volcanic pe

Guanacaste Mountains Range

Tempisque River

PAN AMERICAN HIGHWAY

C O

Central M

BELEN

SANTA CRUZ

NICOYA

CARMONA

SAMARA

CANAS

Gulf of Nicoya

PUNTARENAS

NORTH AMERICA

COSTA RICA

Pacific Ocean

Costa Rica is about one-170th as large as the U.S.
It lies between Nicaragua and Panama in Central America.
It has about 1,425,000 people (more than 90 of every 100 are F
San Jose is the capital and largest city. Limon, on the Caribbea
banana-shipping port, and Puntarenas is the principal Pacific po

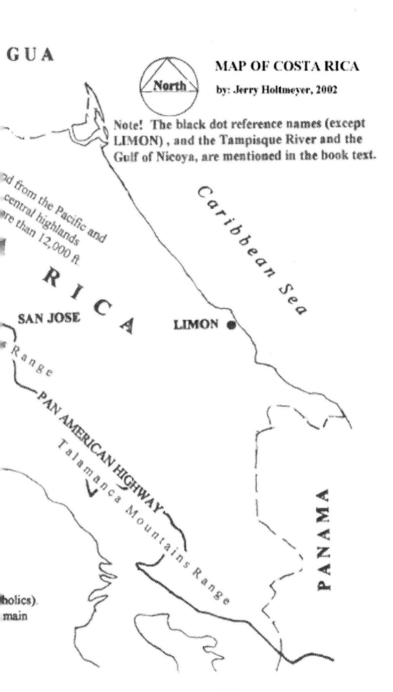

G U A

MAP OF COSTA RICA

by: Jerry Holtmeyer, 2002

North

Note! The black dot reference names (except LIMON), and the Tampisque River and the Gulf of Nicoya, are mentioned in the book text.

nd from the Pacific and central highlands re than 12,000 ft.

Caribbean Sea

R I C A

SAN JOSE

LIMON ●

Range

PAN AMERICAN HIGHWAY

Talamanca Mountains Range

PANAMA

holics). main

CHANGES

The vastness

and sparse

vegetation

of Texas

gave way

to the

lush blue greens

of the

tropics

and the

soft lyrical

sounds

of the Spanish

language.

Chapter VI

Across the Mountains to Puntarenas

The sun shone brightly as we left San Jose and started up the mountain to Puntarenas. Another whole new world opened up before us: We traveled through low clouds that produced a shower; after the short shower, the sun sparkled on the clear water splashing over the boulders in the streams. Coffee plantations and sugar cane fields surrounded us.

The stores in the little villages we passed through reminded me so much of those in our country at the turn of the century. However, here, bright colors of paint made them all look gay and festive: green, red, black, blue, yellow—all the colors in one building.

Thatched roof huts clung to the mountainsides; patches of corn or sugar cane grew between the huts. The cows hung onto the mountainsides for dear life. I was born in Missouri, and Terry always talked of me walking with a list because of the hills there, but this had anything in Missouri that I ever saw beat off the map. All along the way, cute little faces with big brown eyes and little boys with bare bottoms greeted us.

Now, off in the distance, we could see the Gulf of Nicoya, just a glimpse though, and then up more mountains and down again. As we came down the last one, we crossed a bridge over a wide river flowing into the Gulf. To the left stretched the road into *Puntarenas* (Point of Sand), to the right, the road onto the Peninsula. Soon, we would travel the latter to our home in Nicoya.

We came to the *Cabinas Orlando*, located on the beach of the Gulf of Nicoya, a few miles from the city of *Puntarenas*. We occupied the largest cabin available. It had ample room for our family. The cabin had a kitchen, so I could do my own cooking again.

Brigid saw the stove with the oven as we walked in.

"Are we going to have home-made bread again?"

"I don't think I'll try that here; we won't be here very long, Brigid."

A screened-in porch served as one of the bedrooms in the cabin. We always found small lizards in this room, and never determined how they managed to get in. This unnerved the children and me at first, but we learned to live with them. In fact, we got to know them individually, and we became good friends: one special little fellow, *Pancho*, larger than the rest, lived on the front patio. He waited for me to come outside and then went up onto the branch of the tree and watched me hang out diapers.

Unfortunately, however, when I think of *Puntarenas*, I associate it with sick children. First of all, Camille got diarrhea. She was nine months old. Everything she drank or ate came right back out in her diaper within a short time. Even with this problem, she didn't cry or fuss: she'd look up at me and smile sweetly. That made my heart ache. I boiled the water and everything I used, but that didn't seem to help. Her sickness necessitated my first trip to the hospital in search of the doctor, Sanchun by name.

"I must go into the city to take Camille to see a doctor," I told the children one morning.

"How will you know where to go?" asked Hilary.

"I talked with John, and he told me what bus to take."

When we arrived at the hospital, I just stood there looking at it for a while. A wall surrounding the building confronted me. Broken bottles of all sorts were cemented to the top of the wall with their jagged edges pointed upward: Among these jagged edges of bottles, buzzards scoped out the place.

I finally got the nerve to walk inside. After checking in with the nurse, we sat on a bench waiting our turn with all the other people sitting there. I looked into their eyes and realized there was an understanding between all of us, despite the difference in language and customs and culture: They looked at Camille and told me with their eyes that they hoped she would be better soon. They knew that sickness is something we all have in common, and consequently we all know the same anxiety. I couldn't help but think all the more how blessed we are in our country with all the latest in equipment to work with. Here it was the bare minimum in many cases. When they called us in, Dr. Sanchun gave me some medicine for Camille; he said that it should take care of the problem.

Here in *Puntarenas* I first tried shopping in the market place for vegetables and fruits. This was something I always enjoyed afterward. The names of the vegetables were so much fun to learn: *zanahoria* for carrot, *repollo* for cabbage, and *papas* for potatoes. A tiny supermarket nearby provided the case of pasteurized milk we used. Chinese people owned most of the shops and stores.

One day as I walked down the main street of *Puntarenas*, looking at the brightly painted wooden houses built right onto the sidewalk, I didn't think I'd like living in a house like that. In the United States, we become accustomed to front lawns, and I didn't think I would like having the house right on the sidewalk. But as I passed one house, the front door opened and I glanced inside. Then I stopped to look inside. Beyond the entrance hall, with its beautiful bamboo furniture and still more beautiful Chinese pictures and carvings on the walls and tables, was an open courtyard: Soft greens, brilliant splashes of color in the various flowers mingled with the birds everywhere. I drew a deep breath and the girl at the door smiled at me as she held the door open until I walked on. I guess I fell in love with the Spanish-type house and will stay in love with them.

On Sundays we went to Mass at the Cathedral in *Puntarenas*, an old, old church; a band played during the entire High Mass. I found it difficult to appreciate that, especially when they played the loudest at the Consecration, the most solemn part of the Mass. At the end of Mass, they marched out of the Cathedral with the celebrants and then paraded through the park surrounding the church and onto the street, quite different from anywhere else.

John came over to our cabin one day and told us he had some bad news.

"We're all going to the hospital tomorrow to receive our second typhoid shot."

That announcement brought some groans from all of us; most of us had had bad reaction from our first typhoid shot.

"I really don't want to get this shot," Bob said. "Remember how sick I got from it in Texas? I had fever, and my joints ached."

"Yes, I remember, Bob, but we don't have a choice."

The next day we all dutifully went to the hospital and received the shot; we experienced the same reactions again. Our cabin looked like a little hospital.

Keeping clean sheets on hand presented a problem; the woman doing the laundry for the cabins and I got together on this: I washed the sheets not stained, she, the stained ones.

To do this, she built a fire amid some stones in the yard alongside the laundry, placed a large kettle on it, and boiled the stained sheets. The automatic washer in the laundry room badly needed repairs; after several attempts to wash our clothes in the washer, I went back to the method drummed up by Martha Clark when we lived in San Jose. The shower stall was tile; we plugged up the drain, filled the water to the little ledge that forms the one side of the stall and then used our feet as agitators: It worked quite well.

With the children sick, I tried to keep fresh fruits and vegetables available. I walked down the road to little wooden market stalls that lined the road. As I bought fruit and vegetables, if I didn't know the names, I asked them to write them down so I could learn the Spanish words. No matter where I went, older people as well as the young people could read and write; I felt the level of literacy here surpassed that of the United States. The people prided themselves in their schools. Schools were everywhere. Some were little unpainted buildings with thatched roofs, others were well-kept buildings. Early in the morning, in the city or rural areas, children walked to school in their well-pressed school uniforms. It was very impressive.

The pounding of the surf could be felt in our cabin: It was our constant companion. I didn't, however, grow to love this beach on the gulf. True, it held a strange magic because in imagination, one could see the pirate ships and the early trading vessels coming into the port of Puntarenas, but the water looked dark from the black volcanic sand: We didn't swim there.

It provided startling beauty, though, at times. One evening, somber, almost-green-colored clouds, piled high in the eastern sky; brilliant streaks of lightning flashed through the clouds, and yet a partial rainbow softened the fierceness of it; to the west, the sun set in a blaze of gold and rose-tinted clouds.

The port of *Puntarenas* received all of the heavy equipment shipped to Costa Rica for the project. As it arrived, Terry and Ed and some of the local operators of the Ministry of Transportation drove the equipment to Nicoya.

Terry returned from delivering equipment there one day.

"I've seen our house in Nicoya; it needs some adjustments but I think you'll like it. Nicoya is a neat little town."

"Yeah!" came the reply from all of us.

So we started off on the last leg of our journey to our new home.

John, Terry, and Ed went on ahead of us with some more of the equipment. Rose Murphy and their children left Puntarenas at that time. The following day, the children and I left in a van with Pedro Tirado from the AID Mission in San Jose. Martha Clark and her girls, Laura and Catherine, were in another van.

As we drove along we saw lots of evidence that the Peninsula was cattle country. We stopped at the town of *Canas* for lunch.

"Mom, look at all the cowboys on their horses here," Terry said as we came into town.

"This looks like some of the western movies at home," added Kevin. "Even the stores and restaurants look like them."

"Look, there's a special window on the side of that building that's a bar; it's just for cowboys. No need to get off the horse when they drink their refreshment," added Bob.

"But the cowboys don't have the big hats like the cowboys at home," observed Rory, "they're much smaller canvas hats and have small brims."

"We'll be learning many new things, I'm sure, while we're living here," I answered as we got out of the van and went into the restaurant.

While there, a Peace Corps worker, who heard about us coming, joined us. She hugged all of us.

"It's so good to see you. I heard quite a while ago that some families from the States were coming."

"Are there other Peace Corp workers here on the Peninsula?"

"Yes, you'll be meeting one who's living in Nicoya."

During lunch we filled her in on some of the news from the States.

Later, as we left the restaurant, she said, "It's been so much fun talking with people from the States. I'll probably be seeing you from time to time."

As we continued our journey, we saw more and more cattle ranches. It really did remind us of the days of the Old West in our country.

"Dad said they have six months of dry and six months of wet weather on the Peninsula. I'm glad it's the rainy season now; it looks like the cattle have plenty of grass to eat," Cronan said.

Along the way, Pedro stopped to make some business calls at some of the ranches, which put us behind schedule; it grew dark and the rain started falling when we finally reached Nicoya: Terry looked relieved when he saw us.

We ate dinner at Hotel Ali. People lined up everywhere on the sidewalk around the Hotel to look in the windows to see us. Some who could speak a little English came and welcomed us to Nicoya. All in all, a gala affair.

Camille and I spent the night at the hotel; Terry made arrangements for me to do that because the house had just been painted and he knew how sick I got from the smell of new paint. Tomorrow, I'd see our new home.

Chapter VII

Set up Housekeeping in Nicoya

Monday morning Terry and the children escorted Camille and me on a tour of the town of Nicoya. The church and its courtyard were the center of the town. *Quioscos* lined the sidewalks bordering the courtyard. They offered for sale all flavors of *frescos*, a fruit and milk blended drink; *pastel de pinas*, a wonderful dessert of pineapple wrapped in pastry; *tortas*, little tortillas wrapped around meat, tomatoes, and cabbage; and all sorts of snacks. The bandstand, located near the church, had sidewalks fanning out from it in all directions. Hotel Ali occupied the west corner across the street from the courtyard. The post office, clinic, and several stores faced the courtyard from the north; stores of various kinds lined the streets across from the courtyard on the east and south sides.

From the hotel, we went down the hill, over the bridge across the Nicoya River, and up the hill to the other side of the river. To the left was the school and straight ahead, the housing project called INVU (*Instituto Nationale Viviendos Urbanization*), the National Institute of Housing and Urbanization where our houses were located. These were houses built for low-income families. Those that we in the project occupied were rented by us for the duration of the USAID Contract. You couldn't miss the project houses in this section: all were painted white, inside and out. All the others displayed bright colors of paint. Our home stood directly across from the schoolyard.

Boxes with all of our belongings from the States, amid the rollaway beds, the portable kerosene stove and kerosene refrigerator greeted me as we entered our home. Terry had to leave, so Terry, Jr., Kevin, Rory, and Bob set about getting the stove assembled.

Two packing boxes set on top each other provided the base for the stove.

"Do you want some water boiling for coffee, Mom?" Kevin asked.

"You bet I do."

He lit one of the three burners on the stove.

"It's been a long time since I smelled kerosene burning. In fact, I was a little girl when I last smelled it."

"We'll need to experiment with the burner until we get the right combination."

"I can see we'll need to learn how to adjust the burner. Look at the cloud of smoke it's sending up."

"I see there's a portable oven that fits over two of the burners— wonder how that will work."

We later invested in a used bottled gas stove which simplified my life immensely.

The refrigerator took some time to figure out. The boys took turns lying on the floor on their stomachs as they tried to determine how to light the kerosene burner in a compartment on the bottom of the refrigerator: They finally managed to get it lit. We found it worked like a charm as long as you kept kerosene in it; we tried to remember to refill the container before it ran out. If we didn't, it meant back on the floor on the stomach again to relight the burner. The refrigerator fascinated all the children because we lit a fire to make the ice form in the freezer compartment and cool the other part of the refrigerator. However, with no thermostat in it, the everyday opening and closing of the door to get food out kept the food from freezing; if we were gone a couple of days, all the food froze.

As we established a routine and completed the unpacking, we enrolled the children in school. We planned to get correspondence courses from the States a little later so the children could stay on their grade level with the States. We wanted them to also go to the local school; the local school schedule of 7:00 a.m. to 12:00 noon left the afternoon for correspondence classes.

Marcia Gross, the Peace Corps worker here in Nicoya, went with us to enroll and introduce the children to their respective classes, Terry and Kevin in the *Liceo de Nicoya*, high school, Rory, Robert, and Cronan in the *Escuela*, grade school, and Sean in the Kindergarten.

All the children wore uniforms of white shirts and navy blue trousers or skirts. Sean's Kindergarten shirt reminded me of the white-tunic type tops that dentists wore in the States. We had no problem finding the right size shirts for the boys, but the pants proved a real problem. We went to all the stores featuring uniforms but found they just didn't stock pants long enough for our boys; the local people were shorter. I remembered when I looked across the schoolyard at recess, I could see our boys' heads over all the other children.

"Mom, there's a boy in school who is an apprentice in a tailor shop," Rory said one day, "he said if you purchased the material for the pants he could sew them for us in his home."

"That sounds like a great idea, Rory. We'll try that."

I bought the material, and Terry, Jr., Kevin and Rory took it to him. He measured the boys and in a few days they had the pants. He did very good work. He also made Terry's work clothes.

Two 50-gallon drums mounted on a stand behind the house contained our water supply; when the city turned on the water for our section of town, the drums filled if there was enough water pressure. We usually got the drums filled during the night. Much of that provided the water needed for washing clothes the next day. Needless to say, we conserved water. When the water flowed, we also filled our three-gallon cream cans, the kind the farmers in the States used for their cream or milk. We boiled this water for drinking and for use in brushing teeth.

Avelina came to help with the washing and ironing. She was: a very pretty young woman, small in stature as most of the people were. She washed in the morning and ironed after lunch. With no machine available, she washed the clothes by hand. It was fascinating to watch her do that in the special *pila*, sink behind the house. Her hands moved swiftly as she scrubbed each piece and sometimes would slap the clothes on a flat rock put in the sink for that purpose. Soon, however, our old metal scrub board used at camp in Wisconsin, unearthed from our packing boxes, replaced the rock. A little skeptical at first, Avelina tried using it; from then on it never left her side. With twelve of us to wash for, she had her hands full. During the six-month rainy season though, she had an understanding with the older boys in the family: If they got their jeans too muddy, they scrubbed the mud off first before they gave them to her. The schoolyard fence, across the sidewalk from our house, served as the clothes line. When she returned after lunch, she gathered the clothes from the fence a little at a time and ironed them: shirts and dresses first, then the rest.

Brigid, Hilary, and Camille were Avelina's special friends. They learned to converse with her very rapidly. She had two children of her own, her boy the same age as our youngest boy, Hilary. She and Hilary became fast friends.

When she came in the morning, Hilary heard her at the sink outside and called to her.

"Avelina."

She had a special little whistle she gave in answer to him; then he would laugh and run out to talk to her and tell her all the news.

When we first arrived, we had electric power from six in the morning until midnight. This raised a little havoc at first because I frequently had to get up in the middle of the night with Camille and relied on candles then. She still had trouble with diarrhea: The medicine prescribed by Dr. Sanchun did not give her the relief we expected.

I took her to his cousin, Dr. Xavier Yockchen, who had his office in Nicoya. He gave her a shot of some sort and a bottle of medicine called *Hostaclini*, to be taken as prescribed. I'll always remember that name. The diarrhea stopped and she started to gain weight. I told him how impressed I was with her rapid recovery.

"Where did you learn how to deal with this type of problem?"

"I graduated from the School of Medicine at the University in Mexico City. I had special training in dealing with diseases in the tropics."

"Thank you, Doctor. I'm so grateful for your help with Camille."

We had found a very good doctor whom I trusted: That's always a must when traveling with a family.

As I mentioned before, I enjoyed buying vegetables because they had such interesting names that were fun to pronounce. I bought mine in Nicoya at a small stall; they patiently taught me the names of the vegetables and fruits I was not acquainted with. In the stores, I looked for brown sugar and molasses for baked beans—*dulce* was a good substitute for both: sugar cane, put into the machine, came out in liquid form which poured into a mold to harden.

We bought bananas from a young man who sold them door to door from his little cart; he came early in the morning so we would have them for breakfast. We usually bought twenty, sometimes thirty if we wanted to bake banana bread. In orange season, a man came on horseback with a one-hundred-pound sack of them; we picked out what we wanted. Vendors came with avocados also, delicious on fresh warm corn tortillas with a little salt sprinkled on them.

One of my favorite stops on my way to the market in the morning was at the very tiny home of our Costa Rican "Aunt Kate." We called her that because she reminded us of our Aunt Kate in the States. She had lived many hard years, too, and certainly without many conveniences, and yet she walked proudly and erectly. She took particular pride in her washing. Her son taught at the school and always wore white shirts. Her own small yard had a few flowers but no grass. She laid her starched, white clothes in the sunlight on the nice green grass in the yard across the street, and watched until they were ready for ironing. Even during the rainy season, the sun shone part of the day, usually just long enough to dry the clothes. But what always remained a profound mystery to me was how the clothes remained clean despite the people on horseback passing by on the muddy street. But stay clean they did, and they remained spotless also throughout her ironing process.

The iron she used had a small grate on the bottom into which she placed tiny hot coals to heat the bottom. Vents on the sides above and below the grate allowed the smoke to escape, yet I never saw a smoke smudge on any of her clothes. We always learned something new when we visited her.

In setting up housekeeping, we had to make the best of a small house and come up with a study room so the boys could do their correspondence school work at desks.

That necessitated making triple-deck bunk beds in one room. Kevin took over that project.

"Mom, the only place with enough space to work is in the living room."

"I see no problem with that."

Little did I know beforehand the outcome of that project. Kevin started using the electric drill, and the noise of the drill attracted all the neighbors. One after another they asked permission to enter. I could hardly walk through the room filled with inquisitive folks who had never seen an electric drill before; they followed him into the bedroom where he assembled the bunk beds. This also fascinated them because they had never seen beds built on top of each other. Kevin finished off the beds by disassembling the rollaway beds and using the springs and mattresses from them on the bunk beds.

Marcia, the Peace Corps worker, came up in the evening.

"Everyone in town is talking about what the *Gringos* make for beds. I had to come and see for myself. That's a neat idea. Your family is making quite an impression here, and that's good."

We were briefed in advance to look out for scorpions, snakes, and the like. One evening, as the children and I sat in the living room, a scorpion came crawling merrily across the floor, his tail curled ever so neatly on his back. He went right by Camille sitting on the floor. Bob recovered enough from the shock to run over and kill it. This incident made me feel just a little uneasy, especially because Terry wasn't home.

During the night, I awakened from something crawling on my foot. Before thinking, I shook it violently and it felt as though I stuck my big toe into an electric bulb outlet. The sounds I emitted woke everybody in the house.

Terry, Jr., came running into the bedroom.

"What's happened, Mom?"

"Something bit my big toe, I don't know what."

We looked around and found a scorpion near the bed. What do we do now? What would happen to me? So far, other than severe swelling in the area of my toe, I had no other reaction.

"I think you'll be all right, Mom, if you don't feel sick now."

"I guess you're right. I don't think I'll wear a shoe on that foot for a while, though."

In all the confusion, I thought I heard music and singing somewhere nearby.

Kevin came into the room with a grin on his face.

"Mom, three musicians are serenading the young girl next door."

"At this hour of the night?"

"It's probably at the request of her boyfriend."

Well, they saw activity at our house so they came over and began to serenade us too—what a lovely way to end our day of the scorpions.

During the first few months, rows of little children looked through the screens into our dining room to see what we did and what we ate; some sat in the branches of the tree in front of the house so they could get a better view of our table at mealtime. When the boys leveled the tiny yard in front of the house, they had to take care not to poke the little ones standing around watching them.

We learned quite suddenly that we truly lived in cattle country. Our six-year-old son, Sean, returning home on the road from the town, heard a loud noise behind him. As he crossed the river, he looked back and saw a herd of cattle, driven by *vaqueros*, coming down the road toward him. He saw a small *quiosco* nearby, ran to it, and climbed to the top as the herd went by. No one tended the *quiosco* at that time of the day. Alone at the top, he had no idea how he got up there and didn't know how to get down.

At home, Rory heard the sound of the cattle and the calls of the *vaqueros*, and he went down the sidewalk to check it out.

"Sean, how did you get up there?" he shouted as he ran to rescue him.

Sean, still shaking, fell into Rory's arms; he still held on to Rory's neck as they came into the house. From then on, one of the older boys always went with the younger ones on the road to town.

Dad's arrival home in the Jeep was always heralded by the hollering of the monkeys living in the trees along the river. Somehow, they never accepted the sound of the Jeep engine into their world. This time when Dad arrived, Sean told him the story of his encounter with the cattle drive.

"I know just how you felt, Sean. I had to run for my life, too, the other day A herd of cattle came down the road we were working on; the *vaquero* had a rope on one cow. She was mad at the world and anyone in sight. She came straight for me. The *vaquero* whistled and hollered to me because he knew he couldn't control her before she hit me. The only place I could see was a telegraph pole with a fence alongside it. I squeezed between the pole and the fence, and that saved my day. It's a good thing I'm thin. After the cow missed me, she went after the *vaquero*. She stuck her horn onto the rump of his horse, and the last I saw was all three of them riding hard into the sunset."

"Gosh, Dad, you have a good guardian angel, too; that's what Mom said I had."

Eventually, we settled down into a routine of schooling, shopping, and basic language obstacles.

BACK IN TIME

From jets and cars

to

horses and oxcarts

we journeyed

to a

slower pace

of life

with time

to savor

the richness of

the little

ordinary

miracles of life.

Chapter VIII

President of Costa Rica and US Ambassador Come to Nicoya

We finished October off with a Halloween dance at *Rancho Alegre*. The *gringos*, their favorite term for us, were the guests of honor. Martha and I had fun making the costumes; the kids enjoyed seeing us get dressed up the evening of the dance.

"Mom, it's still raining very hard; how will you and Martha get to the Jeep without ruining the crepe paper parts of your costume?"

"We can use some of those large pieces of plastic sheeting stored in the closet. That should keep us intact."

We managed to get into the Jeep unscathed; now we wondered if the river we needed to fjord would be too high to get through: We barely made it. We enjoyed learning to dance to their music. They held a contest for the best costumes. Martha and I won first prize: a barbequed chicken, Costa Rican style.

In November we received word that the President of Costa Rica and the U.S. Ambassador planned to come to Nicoya to take part in signing agreements on the work to be done on the Peninsula through the USAID project. The agreement was among the government of

Costa Rica, USAID, and the Association for the Development of the Peninsula of Nicoya for the general development of the Peninsula. ITAF's part in the agreement was to train local operators and mechanics here on the Peninsula to operate and repair heavy road building equipment. Up to now, operators and mechanics came from San Jose to do the work. The Association agreed to provide food for the trainees and to pay for repair parts for the equipment.

We looked forward to attending the meeting in the park. To prepare for this, I bathed Camille in the sink behind our house. This may sound a little unusual but we used the sink to do the family washing and to give baths to the little ones when there wasn't enough water in the drums for them to take a shower.

Just as I rinsed Camille, the call came through the house.

"Mom, Ambassador Raymond Telles is coming down the sidewalk to see us."

I took Camille and wrapped her in her bath towel. With her hair still dripping wet, I walked into the living room with her to meet the Ambassador.

"You're doing very well here."

"Yes, we are. In fact, we're really enjoying it."

"I'd like our photographer to take a picture of us if you don't mind."

"That's fine with me if *you* don't mind Camille's informal attire."

"That's the way I want it."

The photographer took the picture of the Ambassador playing with Camille wrapped up in her towel. After a short visit, they left, and we proceeded on with our preparations.

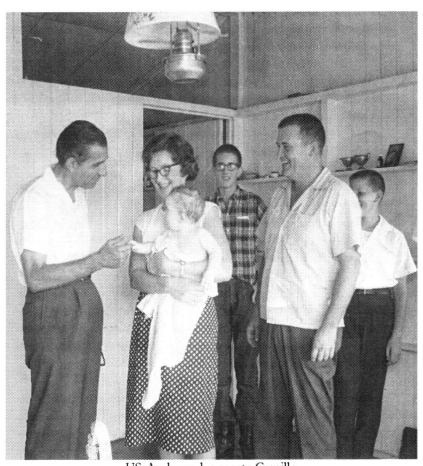

US Ambassador meets Camille

Terry sat with the dignitaries on the podium, so we wanted to get there on time. As we came up the street, we saw the President of Costa Rica walking to the park, dressed very informally, with only a few people walking with him. It seemed so strange to see him go to an affair such as this with such little pomp and circumstance.

After the ceremony I walked with the children to the hotel to get a cold soda. The President, Francisco Orlich, came out of the hotel just then walked up to me and shook my hand.

"I assume you are the mother of the family of ten children associated with the USAID Program."

"Indeed, I am."

"I'm pleased to have your family here in Costa Rica; I hope you will have an enjoyable stay with us."

"Thank you very much, Mr. President; I'm sure we will."

He shook hands with each of the children before walking away. It had been quite an exciting day!

With rain every day, we soon found it necessary to pour a cement patio around our sink at the back of the house or lose someone in the mire. We hired a man who did the cement work on most of the houses.

"Look, there's an ox cart coming up the sidewalk," shouted Chris one morning. Everyone came running out to see it.

"It has a load of gravel for the patio."

What a change to see an oxcart instead of a dump truck doing that kind of work. The children watched, completely fascinated, as the man used a small stick to touch the oxen near their heads to steer them in the right direction. The pair of oxen just barely fit between our house and the house next door. The cart and the yoke for the oxen were painted with a beautiful, colorful design unique here on the peninsula. The owners took great pride in caring for their carts; an artisan kept busy full time painting these designs on carts.

We looked forward to each load of supplies brought to the house; we learned that the young oxen were paired with a rope about 3 feet long between them, so they lived that way until they retired; when the oxen retire to the pasture, they still walk together, without the rope, side by side everywhere, just as they did when under the yoke.

November came and Martha planned on having our first Thanksgiving dinner at her house. She asked the people at Hotel Ali to bake the turkeys for her in their oven since she didn't have one large enough to accommodate the birds.

She ordered two turkeys from a local farmer and told him to bring the *dressed* birds to the hotel the day before Thanksgiving. There must have been a breakdown in communication, however, because on Wednesday, the farmer brought two live turkeys up the sidewalk about sunset.

He reached our house first.

Rory took one look at the turkeys. "Mom, you gotta' come and see this."

"What in the world can we do with this live turkey? We can't dress it tonight or tomorrow. Please tell him we can't take the turkey."

"He said one turkey went to our house and one turkey went to the other American house; he's bringing the other one to Martha."

That bird spent the night penned up in our kitchen, looking as bewildered as we did. I never did know what Martha did with the other one.

In the morning, Terry, Jr., Kevin, and Rory took the turkey outside; they tried their hand at killing it with a machete. Needless to say, killing the bird turned into quite an experience!

When the boys pronounced the turkey dead, we used the water I boiled to defeather it. Now to dress it! I remembered helping my aunts on the farm dress chickens, but I never dressed one by myself, much less a turkey. I went to Maria, one of our neighbors, asking for help. When she came into the house and saw the turkey on the dining room table, she gasped for breath. She never dealt with a turkey either. Together we struggled along and finally declared it ready for roasting. That was one turkey neither of us will ever forget!

The turkey went to the hotel for roasting; they told us to pick up the roasted bird at 3:00 p.m. I volunteered to cook the potatoes. At three o'clock, when we went to Martha's house, we had a huge pot of mashed potatoes. She had some vegetables and a salad: the boys came back empty-handed from the hotel; the turkeys were not done yet. No husbands had arrived either.

"Martha, let's eat what we have while it's still warm."

"I guess we might as well. Thanksgiving isn't a national holiday here, so the men will probably come home later."

We didn't have a family dinner as we planned, but the turkey did arrive in time for dessert.

The men came through the house to eat at one time or another, but each left again to go back to the job sites: John and Ed to Nandayure, surveying the road up the mountain to Vista del Mar, Terry to work on the road to Santa Ana.

Martha and I sat at the table with our last cup of coffee.

"Well, at least we can say we tried."

"It's the thought that counts, Martha."

In the wee hours of the morning of December 12, we awakened to very loud noises echoing off the mountains near our home. It sounded like bombs exploding from the direction of the town. My first thought coming out of a deep sleep was, *Someone's invading the country. How will I defend our children without Terry?* The explosions continued. Why weren't people running about? No one moved anywhere. We stood in the living room in utter amazement. After a while, the explosions stopped: silence everywhere.

As dawn broke, everything around seemed to be very normal.

"Kevin, why don't you go into town and try to find out what happened."

"Okay, Mom, I'll go."

He came back with a smile on his face.

"You're not going to believe this, Mom. Today is the Feast of Our Lady of Guadalupe. They start celebrating the feast by shooting off their home-made bombs from a pipe in the church courtyard around 3:00 a.m."

"Well, that's a completely new experience for us. We didn't celebrate that Feast like that in the States: I don't think we'll forget this celebration very soon."

It was time now to look for Christmas presents for the family; I talked with the older boys about toys for the little ones.

"I've looked for toys but haven't found any I liked. Maybe you can look around for some too."

"I've seen some homemade wooden toys at the Cooperative that I'm sure they'd like," said Cronan.

"I'll check that out next time I'm in town. That sounds great."

Consequently, I bought little wooden ox carts, a stick horse with a beautifully carved head, some corn husk dolls, and even a little wooden road-building scraper: perfect gifts.

Christmas came and with it, the same expectation of waiting for Jesus to come. The shepherds, gathered around the crib, looking in at Baby Jesus, Mary and Joseph there with the cow and donkey lying contentedly beside them, everything the same as other years. It felt strange, though, to walk to church without coats instead of being bundled up in the car driving through snow drifts. But the Mass for the feast was the same as those celebrated anywhere in the world. Peace and contentment filled us as our family took part in the Mass.

The little ones loved the gifts that Santa left them. The basket of red delicious apples turned into the big treat for the holiday. We could buy all kinds of fruit any day: oranges, mangos, papaya, bananas, but Christmas brought apples to the market. It was the only time we saw them.

A very special Christmas gift for the family arrived by mail from the States. Grandpa McCarthy sent a tape of songs he used to play on the guitar and sing to the children at home. In earlier years, he sang tenor with a barbershop quartet and had quite a repertoire of songs, some Irish and some from World War I where he served as a marine. What a gift of love! It was just like having him with us for the holidays. We still have the tape. All the children have a copy of it and treasure it.

In January, John and his family had to return to the States; it was a sad time for everyone. Terry took John's place as field director; this meant that, now with only two families left, we saw less and less of Terry. He spent quite a bit of time at first in San Jose.

He needed some typing done there so he radioed the Association to ask me to come to San Jose with my typewriter. This typewriter, a portable Hermes, was my pride and joy.

The next day I caught the bright and early, and only flight into San Jose; today, a small plane, a Beech 18, came instead of the usual C46. All the seats in back were taken, but the pilot insisted I could sit in the right seat up front in the cockpit with him.

We started down the dirt runway, and just before takeoff, the plane sort of ground looped, and we were heading straight for the fence on the side of the field. I put my hands over my eyes and waited for the crash. Suddenly, we whirled away from the fence and ended up where we started from but facing the opposite direction.

The pilot turned the plane around; he told the man who opened the door to check the baggage compartment; he said it wasn't loaded right. They shuffled the baggage around, the door again closed, and we took off.

As we came to our first stop, Santa Cruz, I could see the people sitting by the field waiting for us to land. At the last minute, though, the pilot gunned the engine for a missed approach and went around again. We barely cleared the palm trees as we turned; I felt I could have reached out and touched the palm fronds. As we came around, we lined up with the runway again and this time we landed. From there we went to Canas and had an uneventful landing. When we landed at Coco International, the passengers inundated the personnel of Lacsa with their stories of all that happened.

I went to get my luggage; my precious Hermes had a big dent in the cover. The very solidly built heavy typewriter had to have received a terrific jolt to put a dent in it. The personnel at the airport told me I needed to go to their main office in the city to report the damage.

At the hotel, Terry met me.

"What in the world happened? You look like you're ready to fight someone."

I showed him the typewriter.

"I wouldn't want to be in the Lacsa office when you go in with that."

"Do I look that bad?"

"Well, you're sort of overprotective of that typewriter."

I then told him about the whole flight; he hugged and kissed me again.

"Thank God you are here. Never mind the typewriter."

I took the typewriter to the Lacsa office.

"We're very sorry about the damage; we'll take out the dent as best we can; that's all we can do."

"I want the broken knob on the left side of the carriage replaced."

"We cannot get a replacement for that here. We're sorry."

I could still use it, so I had to be content with that; it turned out many a letter and report after that. I still occasionally use it just for old time's sake.

When I arrived home after this trip, Rory hugged me as I got off the plane. He had tears in his eyes.

"Mom, when you almost crashed on takeoff the other day, I just knew you would get off the plane. I couldn't believe you went on with that pilot. I thought I would not see you alive again."

"Oh, Rory, I'm so sorry I frightened you so much."

He grabbed my bag and typewriter, and we went home together.

We knew the children couldn't keep up to grade level in the local school. The school did not have text books; notes taken during class provided their only source of reference: The children didn't have that kind of knowledge of Spanish. That concerned Avelina; she told me she could dictate and teach them Spanish while ironing in the afternoon. They all gathered, sitting on the floor around her ironing board in the afternoon and learned Spanish much better.

We still needed to keep up with the lessons they would have back in the States. We made inquiries regarding correspondence courses from the States; we chose the courses from The Calvert School in Baltimore,

Maryland.

Near the end of January, Avelina gave birth to her son, Jose. He was just like an addition to our family. Another lady came to do the washing the few weeks of Avelina's absence. When she returned to do the washing again, she was very upset: Camille's diapers had some stains in them. She soon had a pot of water boiling on the stove with the diapers in them. Avelina did not tolerate any stains on the clothes, particularly on the baby clothes. The older boys told her she wore out their clothes by insisting on taking all the stains out, but she did not relent.

In the dry season, many times the water drums did not have enough water to do the wash. Then all the women went to a place in the Nicoya River called "the sink" to do their washing. Avelina wound a towel in a tight circular fashion on the top of her head; then swung the basket of clothes up on her head and went off to the river. She had graceful movements to accomplish this. I could imagine what I would look like doing that myself.

One day when she prepared to go to the river I told her I would take her there in the Jeep; it happened to be available that morning. As we drove along we saw other women walking with their baskets on their heads, so we stopped and picked them up. We were off again, everyone chatting merrily; we drove a mile before we reached the spot where they washed. The clear, clean water poured over huge boulders into a basin here; some clothes already lay stretched on the rocks along the banks to dry.

By late afternoon Avelina still hadn't returned. I began to worry, wondering what had happened to her. I did not have the Jeep so I couldn't go to look for her. She finally came and I saw tears in her eyes because of the weight of the clothes; no word of complaint came from her but that never happened again. The older boys helped her carry the clothes in the morning and went back in the afternoon to help carry the clothes home.

During these months, Terry, John, and Ed had worked on a road designated by the Association, the road from Santa Ana to Belen. December 11, the road from Santa Ana to Belen was completed. At one time it had been a good road, but from lack of maintenance it washed out every rainy season, and was passable only with Jeeps during that time. They widened the road and cut drain ditches deeper; they made recommendations to the local people on how to improve on drainage and maintain the existing drainage.

While working on this road, Ed found out that the monkeys watched their camp site. One day, alone there for a short period of time, he purchased some fruit from a passerby. Very shortly after, a rather large group of monkeys paid him a visit and all unattached things such as nuts, bolts, shoes and fruit caught their interest. Using some ingenuity, he recovered everything but the fruit.

December 20, they moved the equipment to the next job site at San Lazaro: this road was not as long as the first. The first students arrived January 3 and moved into the camp site at San Lazaro with them. February 25 saw the completion of that road. The equipment then moved to the next site: the road from Arado to Santa Cruz.

Now the dry season was in full swing, and our thoughts turned to ways to seek relief from it. We did what the local people did: go to the beach.

ITAF motor grader on the road from Santa Anna to Belen

Chapter IX

Playa (Beach) Samara

The first week of February the children and I went to *Playa Samara,* a beautiful beach on the Pacific shore of the Nicoyan Peninsula of Costa Rica. In January and February, with the dry season at its height, the thought of lying on the beach by the ocean is irresistible. So one day you find yourself, with all the children, walking across the empty school yard (the school closes during this time) to the road beyond to catch the bus going to *Samara.* Busses, an integral part of life on the peninsula because of the lack of cars, were a source of wonderment to me. I don't know what kept them running or what held them together. We could hear the bus coming long before we saw it, with the rumbling of the engine, with fenders and door rattling.

Terry couldn't go with us at the time so he bade us goodbye as we took the last remaining seats on the bus. The day before the people elected a new President of Costa Rica, Trejos Fernandez, and many of them from outlying parts were returning home after casting their vote, hence the crowded bus. Camille and I took the seat behind the driver, replete with diaper bag and bottles. It startled me when the driver made the Sign of the Cross before starting away. Before we arrived at our destination two hours later, I wondered why we hadn't said the Rosary!

Our journey took us through valleys, mountains, jungle, and rivers.

At some places alongside the mountainside, as I looked out the window to the rear of the bus, I saw that the narrow road did not fully accommodate the outside dual wheel of the bus. This was a little unnerving.

The first stream we crossed boasted a bridge; we caught our breath as the wheels inched over the rather rickety boards; we wondered at its ability to hold up as it did. Each little cluster of thatched roof houses we came to boasted a little store where passengers departed and others waited to ride on to another cluster of houses. Each one of these clusters had a school with the soccer field alongside it.

At one of the stops, we looked for a restroom: toilets with a path. I asked the owner if we could use it; getting an affirmative answer we started out but soon I heard someone call.

"*Senora, Senora!*"

A little girl ran toward us with a roll of toilet paper: an expensive item here. We returned it to the store on the way back to the bus.

With the passing of time, the heat grew more intense. The dust began to swirl in the open windows, covering everything and everyone inside with a fine layer of dust: on the face, hair, eyelashes, and clothes. It appeared as though a make-up artist had transformed everyone's face for roles in a stage play, all of us looked so different.

Before starting up the first mountain, the driver stopped and got out of the bus. He crawled underneath it and checked the steering mechanism and then returned and proceeded on. A little farther on, he stopped again to replace a bolt on the front end.

At this stop, Sean called out to me.

"Mom, look at the size of that hewn log: it's huge!" (The standard size was one meter x one meter x two meters long.)

"It really is big; I wonder where they use them or how they transport them."

"I've never seen anything like that at the saw mill in Nicoya, Mom."

"We'll have to find out what they do with these. That's very interesting."

On another mountainside, we confronted a large truck as we rounded a corner. The helper on our bus, who collected fares and helped the driver with repairs, got off the bus and went over to the truck; soon he walked alongside it and directed the driver, as he slowly began a reverse trip to a turnout where two vehicles could pass. We resumed our ascent, and as we passed the truck, the passengers and driver called out well wishes and farewells to the truck driver before we continued on our journey.

After climbing a few more mountains, we came to the larger river crossings in the jungle, a much cooler but rougher ride. On this part of the trip the clearings and houses were fewer and were far between. At one stop, a woman ran from the house with two glasses of milk for the driver and his helper; it seems they just enjoyed seeing the bus come by. It only ran a few months of the year, because during the rainy season, the river became a raging torrent; it tore out the existing roads, deposited debris of all kinds in its wake, and left the parts in between a sea of mud. Each dry season a dozer and operator from the Road Ministry in San Jose came to make the road passable again for those wishing to go to the beach for a holiday. (One of the local men whom Terry trained was able to do that work the following year.) Dutifully thanking the gracious lady for the refreshment, the driver started out again.

Suddenly, around a corner, a Jeep loaded with happy vacationers met us; out of necessity, we cut a new little road off to the side of the existing one. As we came alongside the Jeep, everyone smiled and waved and called out wishes for a happy journey. The bus had four-wheel drive, so without too much difficulty, we returned to the main road.

Soon after that, a passenger excitedly pointed out of the window. "Look, I see water."

I'm sure Columbus sighting land couldn't have felt more delight than we felt in sighting water. We turned the corner and the whole expanse of ocean and white sand beach stretched out before us: what a gorgeous sight to hot, dusty, tired travelers!

We passed a row of tiny houses and parked in front of the *Pension de Carmen*. Carmen graciously welcomed everyone; our first order of business: a coke to wash down the dust.

In a few minutes, all of us, clad in swim suits, washed off our film of dust in the Ocean. Standing there, awed by the beauty that God lavished on us, the trip seemed short and well worth it. The miles of uncluttered beach stretched off in a semicircle to the left until it reached the rocky point in the open sea. To the right was a sheer cliff with waves sending spray far up to wash it clean. Terry, Jr., Kevin, Rory, Bob, Cronan, Sean, and Christopher rode the nice breakers coming in. We limited Brigid, Hilary, and Camille to about fifteen minutes at a time near the water. With skin that fair we needed to take care. The little ones and I took cover on the verandah and just let the beauty and vastness of the scene completely engulf us.

The short and splashy waves near shore soon invited Brigid, Hilary, Camille and I to come and play again, so we returned to the water. As I watched the children, I saw larger waves breaking over a reef quite a distance out toward the horizon. *They too laughed and played, trying to see who could send their spray the highest. Then one wave sprayed high over the reef and seemed to say, "I see little children playing in the sand," and giggling merrily, slipped back into the sea.*

The blue of the water reminded me of the lakes in northern Michigan but in February up there, ice covered their blueness—here palm trees, not pine trees, lined the shore.

The going rate at the *Pension* included three meals a day; an eager troop waited for each meal, even though most meals consisted of beans and rice. Swimming and exploring gave all of us a ravenous appetite. I'm sure the cook never thought that one family could ever possibly eat that much and still pass an empty dish back for more.

The *gringos* always did things a little differently. We asked that the drinking water be boiled. Several times, I noticed one of the cooks in the kitchen get a little curious and take a taste of the boiled water and spit it out!

In the main part of the kitchen, a specially built stove handled most of the cooking; a heavy wooden frame held baked clay sides which rounded off at the top into which were fitted heavy metal pieces and disks similar to the old wood burning kitchen range used in the States on the farm. The large pots of soup and beans simmered there during the day. Outside, under a shelter, a stove built along the same lines but without the metal parts, held hot, fast fires to cook tortillas and coffee in the morning: one or two small pieces of wood had water boiling in no time at all.

Very early in the morning, before daylight, the cooks prepared the tortillas; a candle provided the light for this work. With a hand grinder, they ground the crude corn. This corn had soaked in water mixed with ashes (lye) all night. The lye mixture loosened the hull of the corn so it could then be rinsed away: it was rinsed many times before grinding. The grinder, similar to the old metal hand grinders used in the States years back, ground and reground the corn three times; a little water added to this enabled the cooks to form the tortillas, all of them perfect and uniform in size. The tortillas were fried on the hot fire in a heavy skillet with no shortening used. They were superb tortillas—we have never found their equal since then.

The workers in the kitchen found it a little difficult to accept the fact that I sterilized the bottles, fed Camille and washed diapers and clothes. All the other families with small children staying there brought along a maid who did that work for them. Every one of the girls working there approached me at one time or another while I did the washing or while I prepared Camille's bottles in the kitchen and asked me if I wanted them to do that work for me here and back in Nicoya.

They found it more difficult to accept the fact that the older boys took care of their "charges," one of the little ones, helping them when it came time to eat, taking them for the trips to the outside toilet or preparing them for bed. One of the boys stayed with them also when I went swimming or exploring.

Dona Carmen said to me one day, "They really love those little ones."

Some of the local girls always watched me when I washed clothes to see if I really knew how. The washing sink here resembled the one at our home in Nicoya where I learned how to wash by watching Avelina. I wished I had taken the scrub board along though; here I used the rock placed in the sink to do the scrubbing: raw knuckles betrayed the fact that I didn't do the washing all the time. Brigid and Camille learned the art from Avelina too and often washed their doll clothes that way later on. I enjoyed watching them pound the little clothes on a stone to get the heavy dirt out.

The water from the sink drained down a little open ditch through the dried mud yard and down into a gully. Many a time the pigs found this irresistible and grunting contentedly, sloshed along through the ditch until someone working there spoiled it all and with much flurry chased them off. The chickens fared much better and had the run of the entire yard. Some of the ashes from the cooking fires were placed in a pile in the yard. This provided chickens a place to periodically get into to dust themselves: that rid them of lice. In the late afternoon, little wooden ladders, placed so they rested on the branches of the trees in the yard, gave the chickens a way to walk up and roost on the branches during the night. However, we noticed that some of chickens turned up missing when we enjoyed a fried chicken dinner or a rice and chicken dish.

The children always found the yard most enchanting and full of new surprises. One day a monkey noticed something particularly enticing on the ground in the yard. It came sliding down the huge frond of a palm tree to pick it up and then scurried back up the tree. Around noontime, the monkeys took their siesta lying on their tummies on a branch of a tree with their legs draping off the side of the branch.

A huge mango tree grew in the yard, a favorite place for the monkeys at their mealtime. Rory really liked mangoes but the fruit was too high in the tree for him to reach.

"Terry, Kevin, Bob, let's pick up some clods of dirt from the ground and throw them at the monkeys and see what happens."

"Okay, let's try it."

The boys started throwing the clods up into the tree and soon mangoes were flying down everywhere. Rory and the boys laughed as they picked up the mangoes:

"That solved that problem."

The children learned to enjoy the green mangoes, as well as the ripe ones, by putting a little salt on them as they ate them.

Carmen told the children one day that she had a surprise for them; she had sweet dough raising in the kitchen.

"Come, I'll show you what I'm going to do with it."

They followed her into the kitchen and watched while she made rolls from the dough.

"We'll wait for them to raise again, and where do you think I'll bake them?"

"There's no oven here in the kitchen," said Brigid.

"Come along and I'll show you."

In the back yard, stood a baked clay, beehive-shaped oven. A fire burned beneath it. When the rolls were ready, Carmen placed the pans on a big wooden paddle and set them in the oven. Soon we enjoyed a special treat.

One morning we saw a ship in the bay; a passage around the left end of the reef allowed the ship to pass through. A boat from the ship came toward the shore. Soon all the children began shouting together.

"Mom, look at the oxcarts coming around the corner. They're dragging those huge logs we saw when we came on the bus."

"I wonder where they're going with them."

"They're heading for the water, Mom!"

"Look, they're floating the logs right out to the boat. The boat can tow them to the ship!"

What an exciting morning! Now we knew how those logs were transported to other places. The ship, called a "Coaster," traveled the coastline. It took the logs to the Puntarenas saw mill. Carmen said she received all her supplies from these ships during the rainy season when the road to Nicoya closed.

One of the pleasant surprises that the ocean held for us was the pools the reef left exposed as the tide went out. These provided endless hours of exploration. All sizes and shapes of pools of crystal-clear water held a myriad of fish and sea life for us to observe. If we sat very quietly for a while by one of the pools, the fish came out from under the rocks and seaweed. Chris and Cronan saw some coming out of hiding.

"Look at that sapphire-colored one, and that red one, and oh, the zebra-striped one!"

"Here comes a bigger gray one; he's sending them all scurrying back to their hiding places."

Rory and Bob went to another pool.

"Look at this rock formation. It's a castle with many spires surrounded by a moat of clear water full of beautiful fish."

"And here is a small, but deep one that looks as if someone scooped it out with a strange special spoon."

In that pool, some little octopi came out from a rock formation. Kevin tried to scoop one up.

"Look, he squirted ink and I can't see him anymore."

"Come on, kids, the tide is coming in; we don't want to get caught here by this rock cliff. We can come back when the tide goes out again."

Terry came on the bus to spend a day with us. As he got off the bus, Brigid laughed when she saw him.

"Your face is dusty just like ours when we came. It makes you look funny."

I looked at him.

"Did you enjoy the ride?"

"Well, did the driver make the Sign of the Cross when you left?"

"Yes, he did."

"We sure did need that and much more didn't we!"

After he had his coke to wash down the dust, he put on his swimsuit and took off for the ocean; then he had that same look of contentment that we had. Now, with Dad here, the boys went out much farther into the water; they had a ball swimming with Dad.

Here again I saw the women very openly flirting with Terry; having *novias* is quite an accepted thing here; it's not done behind a so-called respectable facade, with secret meetings and apartments so the wife doesn't find out. Instead, any man, married or not, is fair game and they use all their charms.

Terry and I would be walking along and meet a woman, and the eyes were just for him, not a cheap selling of themselves solely for a passing pleasure but a frank display of warmth with their full knowledge of fulfillment. To live with and know only one person during your married life is hard for them to understand. Those who eventually realized that this is the way to live respected us for it. This respect led them to notice the greater advantages of such a family unit: perhaps the process of change would be slow, but it was very possible.

Terry took some of the boys for a walk along the full stretch of sand far off to the left. At noon they returned brimming with stories to tell.

"We saw a cluster of beach houses back in the trees similar to houses in the States; they have boats alongside them. One even has an airplane parked by it."

"But we didn't see any people anywhere," said Kevin.

"It was really strange to see an oxcart rumbling along the beach in front of the house with an airplane parked by it," added Bob.

Sean and Cronan broke in with their part of the story.

"We found a real Swiss Family Robinson tree, the size of a big apartment house, throbbing with all sorts of animal life."

"Monkeys, lizards, and parrots chattered away as they went about their work of finding food for the day, in and out among thousands of roots, dark crevices, branches, and leaves."

Probably quite a few remarks also came from the tree directed toward the strange two-legged creatures staring at them from all angles.

At the farther end of the semicircle of beach, they gained access to another beach by crossing through a grove of trees; that beach was smaller and pretty, but not as beautiful as Samara. After lunch Terry took the bus back to Nicoya.

All too soon our vacation ended, too, and we boarded the bus back to Nicoya. Now, we had not only the duffel bags but all the small bags of treasures that the sea had given us: seashells and driftwood, cups the children learned to make from coconut shells, and hearts and minds full of beautiful memories.

The second trip to the *Pension de Carmen* at *Samara* a year later had an extra air of holiday attached to it because Terry went with us. The children had just finished their first Calvert course and that added to it.

Many people on many occasions tried to teach me how to swim but to no avail. Terry tried many times in the various lakes in Michigan, but when it came time to put my head down in the water — I just couldn't do it.

This time I had a new bathing suit, and I wasn't pregnant, so I could find no excuse to give Terry for not wanting to learn to swim. He showed me the fundamentals and let me practice for a while.

"Now, dive in and ride the waves to shore."

"Okay, here goes."

I did exactly that and what a glorious sensation! I had a real ball and felt a sense of accomplishment. I was no Esther Williams for sure, but I was working at it. Once, two large waves broke in succession and all but swamped me. I still have a lot of respect for water.

After the evening meal, the generator cranked up and the bulbs began to glow. Wires stretched across each bedroom with one bulb per room. The rooms had unpainted wooden walls; the windows had no glass or screen: a piece of wood on hinges could be closed and locked with a wooden latch. There were no mosquitoes, so there was no screen. Wooden cots with canvas stretched across them served as beds. In one corner a wooden pole held clothes. Some rooms had a table. The floors were cement: At night crabs clicked their way across the floor. They were very basic rooms but adequate.

Usually one or two of the little children fell asleep at the table in the evening. So after prayers, the older boys put their "charges" to bed. Then Terry and I went out and walked along the beach.

The ocean held still another surprise for us: The brilliance of the blues and whites and gold now change to muted dark blues and silver. We walked along in silence absorbing the beauty. The waves, so mischievous and splashy in the sunlight, now enchanted by the moon, became refined and graceful. With long sweeping movement, they murmured ever so softly in their beautiful ballet; the moon placed a shimmering silver crown on each one, rewarding it for the beautiful performance. Then they broke, oh so slowly, reluctant to lose their precious gift from the moon.

Where does that soft fragrant breeze come from? Perhaps from some far off isle in the Pacific? Looking up at the vastness of the sky with its moon and stars brought back that longing to be with and know the God who lavishes such beauty on his creatures, the beauty we need so that we might be refreshed in mind and body. It refreshes us so that when we look down again and see the needs of so many, we can start working again with renewed efforts.

We said our Office of the Twelve Paters walking along the beach, partly because, more than likely, the generator would be shut off by the time we got back to the room and we couldn't read the Office in the book.

After a week of rest and relaxation, of swimming and exploring, of endless enjoyment in the tide pools, we went on our way back to Nicoya again.

Brigid, Hilary, Camille, and I made a final trip to Samara just after the local school started classes the first part of March. We went for only a couple of days the week before Holy Week, the final big week at Samara. All the stores in Nicoya close and everyone goes to the beach during that week. I don't know how or when this custom started but I didn't like to see it because they observed those holy days commemorating our Lord's Passion with feasting instead of fasting.

It was still dark when we walked to catch the bus; time passed and the sun peeked over the hill. I began to wonder if we had missed the bus; then we heard it coming, all parts of it moving and flapping along. We boarded and were off once again to Samara.

At the first river crossing, we heard a beeping of a horn behind us, so the driver stopped on the other side of the river. A motorcycle came alongside with a young man and girl aboard; the girl got off and came on the bus. She taught school up in one of the clusters of thatched roof buildings in the mountains. This particular Monday morning she missed the bus: The gallant young man saved her day.

We proceeded along, gradually ascending the mountain. We stopped at a little *pension* and some of the people got off the bus; thinking it was a routine stop, I didn't bother to get off. I could see the driver and his helper sitting inside having a cup of coffee. Then the helper came out to the bus, took out some tools and started climbing up to the top of the bus where they kept the tires. I asked him if he needed to change a tire; when he said yes, I decided to have a cup of coffee too. The local children drank a lot of coffee, usually cold; this was a healthier drink than the *frescos* I suppose, because they boiled the water to make coffee; the *frescos* contained unboiled water and the local milk was not pasteurized.

The rest of the trip proved uneventful. It was wonderful to see Samara again. It's hard to say a final goodbye to a place so beautiful. Carmen had difficulty saying goodbye to us because she knew she wouldn't see us again. The rainy season would make the road impassable again and we would be gone after that.

SAMARA

The hot dusty ride

enhances

the beauty

and wonder

of sighting

the sea.

A whole new

world

of delight and exploration

greeted us

to awaken

the feeling

of awe

at the grandeur

of God's creation

Chapter X

Courses from Calvert—School Commences

Terry, Jr., Kevin, and Rory decided to buy a horse after we returned from our first trip to Samara. Living in cattle country, we saw horses everywhere every day; they saw *vaqueros* tending cattle, rounding them up, and driving them to different places, so it came as no surprise that they wanted a horse. Terry told the boys if they found a place to pasture a horse, they could buy one.

They went to the Association office in town and talked to them about pasturing a horse in the area surrounding the *Plantel* where all the road building equipment was kept, a large area of grass surrounded the building. They gave them permission.

Ed Clark, who worked with horses in Texas, told them he would help them look for a horse; they found Patricio on a *finca* (ranch) quite a few kilometers from Nicoya. Terry, Jr., rode the horse home. It was a small horse compared with the western horses in the States, but typical of the horses on the peninsula. The boys grew to love Patricio.

Bob told me one afternoon he wanted to go and check on Patricio over at the *Plantel*. I gave him permission. A while later I heard a scream from Maria who lived at the end of our block; I rushed out to see what

119

happened, and there came Bob with a dead coral snake in his hand: Maria and I were in a state of shock.

"Mom, I came down the wash and this snake was lying there. I went to get a closer look because I'd never seen one with such bright colors; the snake hissed at me, so I picked up a rock and killed it."

"Bob, promise me you'll never do anything like this again; snakes here are very poisonous."

Why was I surprised that the first and only encounter I had here in Costa Rica with a snake came with Bob? The first time he went outside as a toddler in Grand Haven he brought me a little garden snake crawling through his fingers: He was the one in the family who always pushed the envelope.

Terry, Jr., rushed into the house one morning after he went to check on Patricio.

"Mom, Patricio broke through the fence; he's gone and I can't find him anywhere."

Kevin, Rory, and Bob came running into the room.

"We'll go out with you to look for him; he's gotta' be around here somewhere."

A sad-looking bunch came back empty-handed a while later.

Terry was determined to find him.

"May I ask Marcia, the Peace Corp Worker, if I may take her horse to look for him? I think Patricio got lonely for the horses and went back to the *finca* where he lived before."

I didn't know what to do and wondered if Terry would give him permission in this case.

"Well, if Marcia will give you her horse to look for Patricio, you have my permission; but do you remember how to get there?"

"I'll talk to Marcia about it; she knows everything around here."

Terry, Jr., came back to the house with Marcia's horse.

"She knows where the *finca* is and confirmed my directions; I'll see you this afternoon."

Hours passed, and Terry, Jr., didn't return. As it grew dark, I went down into town to look for Marcia; I found her at a *quiosco*; she was not the least concerned.

"He's all right, he'll be back shortly."

A few hours later, panic set in; a storm broke with lots of lightning and heavy rain. Where was Terry, Jr.? Then I heard the clop, clop of horse's hooves coming up the sidewalk. There came Terry, Jr., soaking wet, riding Patricio and leading Marcia's horse: what a wonderful sight!

As he ate dinner, he told us the story.

"I found Patricio back at the *finca* where we got him; I started home riding Patricio and leading Marcia's horse. When it grew dark, I let Patricio find his way through the mountain. Then the storm turned violent. A bolt of lightning rolled down the wash as we approached it, a huge ball of light that lit up the whole place. I'll never forget how it looked! Both horses stopped dead still until it passed, then continued on again. Patricio took me home. I'm so glad to be home again."

Yes, home safe and sound, just tired and very wet.

A week later the Calvert Courses arrived. It was time to put the desks to use which Terry, Jr., had constructed in one room of the house: They lined two walls of the room; he did a great job on them. The room looked very professional. The Calvert School wanted someone outside the family to supervise the work; with no one like that available, it was left up to me.

Now we started the routine of the boys going off to the school across the fence at 7:00 in the morning and then to school at 1:00 in the afternoon in the back room of our house. It wasn't too difficult getting them up early in the morning because living so close to the equator, the sun rose at 6:00 a.m. and set at 6:00 p.m. year round: going to bed early wasn't too much of a problem, either.

Terry, Jr., was in 7th grade, Kevin in 6th, Rory in 5th, Bob, in 4th, Cronan in 3rd, and Sean in the 1st grade: I spent most of the time with Sean. Sometimes, I started cooking the evening meal before I finished working with him; consequently, the Teacher's Manual for the First Grade got splattered in places: I stood the Manual on the shelf above the stove while I cooked and worked with him.

The children had to be convinced that they needed to complete a lesson a day or there would be no play; then, I needed to convince the neighbor children that *our* children were in school in the afternoon: I don't know which proved the more difficult.

Trying to stay awake after lunch when the children did their reading assignment, proved a big problem for me. Many a time I fell sound asleep, and off they went to play outside; after all they couldn't finish their assignment with me asleep. They still kid me about that.

I received a pleasant surprise in the mail one day. Clarence Neider, a distant cousin of mine who lived in my home town at one time, informed me he was now doing the evening news on KMOX in St. Louis. He thanked me for helping him get the break into the business. Then I remembered when I worked for Rush Hughes on KXOK in St. Louis, Clarence asked me to take him with me one day to see what it was all about. He enjoyed the day so much he decided to follow a career in radio.

He lost track of me for years. Then he decided to contact my folks and get my address so he could now thank me. He was so glad he caught up with me.

One afternoon, a teacher from the nearby high school came to the house to ask for help. He started corresponding with a girl in Austria; the letter he received from her was written in English; she didn't know Spanish well enough to write a letter. The children picked up Spanish much better than I did, so with their help as interpreters, we translated the letter for him, then wrote a letter to her from him.

We enjoyed the exchange very much; he came back with more letters and pictures. Then we had pictures to enclose in his letter to her. Living that close to the school gave us the chance not only to help someone like the teacher writing letters but also help students who came during recess periods for help with their English lessons: they also wished to learn to converse in English. This reminded me again that the children are the real ambassadors: It brought back memories of our campout in Wisconsin with the Peruvian family. Here, they were my interpreters and the first line of communication.

Martha Clark later agreed to take one of the children, Cronan, to her house and supervise his lessons: this helped a lot. It took two months of work to give the children the first test. After that we gave a test every month.

The children had time for play every day too; with the school work completed for the day, the yard filled with neighbor children playing cowboy and Indian. One of the neighbors had a TV and they saw the cowboy movies. Our doors were always open, front and back. With no screen doors to slow them down, someone often came running behind me in the kitchen and through the living room to "cut the enemy off at the pass." Sometimes the tree in the backyard was the C46 they piloted as they sat on the branch of the tree; they brought the plane in for a landing at the airport over the top of our roof just as the *Lacsa* planes did every day. The dirt runway of the airport was directly across the schoolyard from our house.

Our children helped round up all the neighbors' chickens that roamed through all the yards during the day. They came to know each one of them and to whom they belonged. They hunted eggs all year round, not just at Easter; they knew where each chicken laid her egg and made sure the right neighbor got the right eggs, and the right chickens in their yard.

Beto Hernandez, with his sunny smile and sparkling dark eyes, Rory's best friend, became part of our family and often ate meals with us. He just loved meat loaf and baked potatoes, or meat and cabbage rolls and home made bread.

Rory told me one day: "Beto thinks you are the best cook in the world."

"I think he is a bit prejudiced. Remember, the first time I saw Beto; you brought him home with his lip swollen beyond recognition from a bee sting; I made a paste of baking soda and water and held it on his lip until the pain subsided. After that, I could do no wrong as far as he was concerned."

I guess Beto's gratefulness for so small a favor stemmed from the fact that he never knew his own mother; she left the family after his birth and never returned: He lived with his grandmother.

And so the weeks and months passed with school in session. We celebrated when we mailed those first tests in; after that we mailed one each month.

SCHOOL IN SESSION

An invisible sign

school in session

from 1:00 to ?

went up

in our yard

each school day.

Silence reigned

until the first

student appeared

ready to play

their lesson done

for the day.

Chapter XI

Start Visits to Dr. Cabezes

Starting the seventh month of my pregnancy, Dr. Yockchen wanted me to begin going to Dr. Cabezas in San Jose for my checkups; he preferred I deliver my baby with better medical facilities than he had. This meant flying into San Jose for the doctor visit and staying at the hotel overnight: we had only one flight a day.

My second trip to San Jose, I had problems because of elevated blood pressure and loss of weight: not a very good combination. As we flew across the mountains, I became light-headed and put my head down between my knees. The co-pilot came out of the cockpit about that time and leaned over to see if I was okay: He looked a little nervous. I made it in all right and took a taxi to the doctor's office. There he told me I evidently had picked up some bug somewhere along the line which caused the loss of weight: he gave me medication for that and the blood pressure. The altitude in San Jose didn't agree with me either, so I spent an uncomfortable evening at the hotel; the next day I was feeling much better.

I received a ticket for the premiere showing of Dr. Zhivago in San Jose; I stayed an extra night and went to the theater the last evening of my stay. A red carpet graced the entrance to the theater; beautiful bouquets of flowers bordered the carpet. I wondered what prompted all of this. I took my seat in the mezzanine and awaited the start of the movie.

Suddenly, I heard the National Anthem of Costa Rica being played so I stood up. The President of Costa Rica and his family entered and took their seats just a row ahead of me: they were the reason for the red carpet treatment.

When I arrived at the airport the next day for the trip back home, the pilots looked a little nervous when they saw me on the plane. I guess they thought I'd be staying in San Jose for the rest of the time; little did they know that they would be seeing a lot of me in the next month or so.

At home in Nicoya during the weeks that followed, it became apparent that our septic tank needed to be cleaned out; the man hired did a good job. He then hired other men, and soon trenches appeared all over the back yard; it looked like a movie lot for a World War I movie; it didn't make sense to me. When Terry came home, he explained what happened.

"Back in Michigan, we had sandy soil and didn't need a large drain field; here we have quite different soil so it is necessary to have many trenches to hold the tile for the larger drain field."

"It looks pretty sad to me right now, but I'm sure the kids can think of some new game to play that requires that type of landscaping."

About the middle of July, as I started my ninth month of pregnancy, we took the whole family to San Jose during their school break. This was the first time the children had visited San Jose since we first arrived; they really enjoyed shopping and sightseeing.

Terry, Jr., Kevin, and Rory shopped for a saddle for Patricio. They had a typical Costa Rican saddle at home: two boards with some leather on them that afforded no comfort at all; they usually rode with only a saddle blanket on Patricio.

"Look at the saddle we bought!" announced Terry, Jr., as they returned from their shopping trip. They had bought a beautiful, western style, hand-tooled-leather saddle. Terry still has it.

The children visited the museum in a bank across the street from the hotel which featured many artifacts of the country. They learned much about the history of Costa Rica there. We went to see the *Teatro Nacional*, inaugurated in 1897. It is a beautiful theater modeled after the Paris Opera. A painting titled, "Alegoria" by T. Villa, 1897 hangs in the lobby. It features all the facets of industry in Costa Rica: coffee, bananas, cotton, and rice, a dryland type rice. The amount of rain here negated the need for flooded fields. They used a copy of that painting on the back side of their five *colones* bill: the Costa Rican bill.

Everyone enjoyed living in the hotel; the older boys especially appreciated going to the dining room to eat with no chores connected with it. The women cleaning the rooms at the hotel became fast friends with Brigid, Hilary, and Camille; they brought them all sorts of things from their homes: homemade toys and home baked snacks. Needless to say, a lot of laundry accumulated each day. One of the ladies volunteered to take it home with her to wash so it would not be so expensive for us.

Roberto Alfaro and two secretaries from the USAID office came one evening to have dinner with us so they could meet the family; we really enjoyed their visit. All in all, we had a great holiday but now it was time to go home.

We took off from San Jose airport and landed in *Canas* for our first stop. Because it was the rainy season, the ground off the runway was very soft and muddy. The pilot made too big a swing around the end of it when he turned the plane for takeoff; the wheels became mired in the mud. They asked the passengers to deplane but told us to stay right there near the plane. The pilots then tried again to get the plane moving but to no avail.

All the passengers gathered under the wing of the plane to get some relief from the sun. At lunchtime, *Lacsa* officials took a few of us at a time to a restaurant in their company jeep. They, in the meantime, contacted someone with a tractor to pull the plane out of the mud.

As we returned from the restaurant, they gave us permission to get back on the plane to await the arrival of the tractor. Among the passengers were the members of a band from San Jose scheduled to play at a big party in Nicoya. They got their instruments and began playing; this put everyone on board into a party mood. Some sang; others danced in the aisle.

I had several pounds of hot dogs, (a real treat we always brought back from San Jose), in my bag. I took them and the buns out—no matter the hot dogs weren't heated. Some of the other passengers followed suit and brought out their food or in some cases, drinks: plenty of refreshments for the party. No one seemed to mind anymore about being stuck in the mud.

But at the height of the party, the tractor arrived and the work began to free the plane from the mud. Seven hours after we arrived in *Canas*, we took off for Nicoya.

When we arrived in Nicoya a small crowd greeted the band members. The late arrival of the band didn't dampen their enthusiasm. They could celebrate to the wee hours now. Maria, our neighbor, waited and watched all day for the plane; she hugged and kissed everybody. She had worried all day that something bad had happened to us.

Now, we started making arrangements for my absence during my stay at the hospital when the baby arrived. Terry, Jr., 15 years old, would have charge of all the children with Kevin, 14, and Rory, 13 his first assistants, Robert, 11, Cronan, 9, Sean, 7 and Christopher, 6 comprised the middle group, Brigid, 4, Hilary, 3 and Camille, 1 were the little ones.

Avelina would do the washing and ironing. Abigail, daughter of my favorite neighbor, Maria, would help with the housework. Young and full of energy, she would need that energy to combat the mud on the tiles in the living room in the rainy season and the dust in the dry season. Maria would help with preparing the meals; so we awaited the arrival of our new member of the family.

Chapter XII

Mary Comes into the World

The morning of the 16th of August, the airline's little pickup truck waited for me at the end of the sidewalk by our home. The *Lacsa* clerk and I drove through the school yard to the airport. Terry walked. As we boarded the old C46 we both knew our baby would come today. We started bouncing down the gravel runway, gained altitude, and went on down the valley to Santa Cruz. We landed on the gravel runway there, and as we came to a stop, I looked at the fence bordering the airport. Tree branches served as fence posts, and some had new leaves popping out.

"Terry, look at those fence posts; they look like the ones Kevin drew in the picture hanging above his desk at home."

"I'm sure Kevin saw many fence posts like that around Nicoya; the ranchers here use those everywhere."

Some people got off, a few got on, and some freight changed places. Terry leaned back in his seat.

"I really enjoy flying in this old war bird; we don't see many of them anymore in the States."

"I like them, too; their engines sound sturdy and dependable."

Airborne again, this leg of the flight took us over the low flats by the mouth of the Tampisque River; we landed again on another gravel runway at Canas. Once again people and freight changed places and with a roar and flap of wings, we took off again. Next stop: San Jose, so we needed some altitude to negotiate the mountains. Terry pointed out the window.

"Look over there to the right; you can see Nicoya and Santa Cruz."

I leaned over to have a look. "They look so tiny and alone out there."

Over to our left, mountains rose above us; soon we could see over the smaller mountains to the higher ones in the Interior. Puntarenas passed under the right wing; the plane turned left up the valley, and the hard-paved long runway of Coco International airport came at us.

We took a taxi in to San Jose in the bright, sparkling sunshine; the mountains, still a little sleepy, shook the fleecy clouds out of their eyes so they could better watch the city and drink in the sunshine.

We shared the taxi with a lady who wished to go to Heredia, near San Jose; we turned off the highway, went up the hill to Heredia, and with that passenger safely on her doorstep, threaded our way into San Jose. We crossed a bridge over a clear, sparkling stream that tumbled over the rocks.

"Look, Terry, someone is bathing down there in the bend of the stream."

"That must be a real eye-opener for them this early in the morning. It's pretty cool out there.

At our destination, Terry checked into the hotel; from there, we went on to the doctor's office. He examined me and decided to start inducing labor right away; he checked me into the hospital. Here, I ran into problems of short carts — the *Ticos* are much shorter than my 5'9" frame; being nine months pregnant made me a little clumsy anyway. Once I set the body in motion, I couldn't change course. I looked at the cart and the table with the articles used for prepping me for delivery standing up against it.

"I think this cart is too short for me," I tried to tell the nurse in the best Spanish I could manage; she smiled and motioned me to lie down. As I swung my legs onto the cart, she grabbed all the articles on the table as my feet hit them: She managed to save them all.

With my length to spread the weight over, it's a little difficult to estimate my weight; when it came time to move me to the delivery room, the first nurse didn't do too well getting the cart in motion; a second nurse came to the rescue. We started out and suddenly they broke into a run and I felt myself going up an incline: We just barely made it with a little panting on the part of the nurses.

In the early afternoon, our new little girl came into the world; I caught a glimpse of her and saw that she had lots of dark hair. They had me in a sitting position while delivering her; now the uterus was left to float instead of forcing it into the pelvis: No excessive bleeding occurred. The doctor wanted me to stay in the delivery room for a while; Terry came in to sit with me.

"The baby is in an incubator; she's having difficulty breathing."

Just then the nurse brought in some broth; Terry started feeding me the broth when the doctor came in to check me.

"You're doing fine, Mrs. McCarthy. No problems here. Terry, please come out with me."

This reminded me so much of Joseph's birth. The same things happened then; I was very concerned.

Terry returned.

"They think it best to have a priest come to baptize our little girl since she's having some difficulty."

He kissed me and squeezed my hand.

"I'll go out and look for a priest. There's none here in the hospital; what shall we name her?"

"I'd like to name her Mary."

"Mary it is then."

He found a Franciscan church a block from the hospital; one of the priests came back with him and baptized her: Mary was made a child of God.

They transferred me to a regular room after Terry left. I knew when he came into the room that Mary was dead; the hurt was there in his eyes. He came over to the bed and took hold of my hand; I felt my whole being melting away but I hung on to his hand. He laid his head on my hand and we cried together; then he looked up.

"But I still have you, Mother, I still have you."

A feeling of peace overwhelmed me then just as it had when Joseph died; he, like Mary, was baptized just a few hours before he died. That certainty that they both were now in the presence of God lifted my heart.

Terry looked up again and I saw the tired lines on his face and the eyes, usually so sparkling and laughing, so tired now. His face brightened then.

"I know—another one went back to God."

Silence fell now, and we let the peace and hope take hold and start to heal the hurt in our hearts.

I lifted Terry's hand to my face.

"Mary is quite an individual, isn't she, with her own special place in our hearts, just like Joe has had all these years. Now we can add her name to the end of our family prayers and say, 'Little Joe and little Mary, pray for us.'"

"That's for sure; remember when we went to Church just a few weeks ago so you could receive the Expectant Mother's Blessing? Those prayers were certainly answered. We both heard her first cry at birth, and I watched Father baptize her a little later."

Terry let go of my hand and left the chair and started walking around in the room.

"The doctor said the cause of death was hyaline membrane."

"That's what Joe died of."

"Yes, I remember. You know, Mother, now we'll have to decide where to bury Mary."

We looked into each other's eyes and knew she would be buried alongside her brother in Baby Land in Grand Haven, Michigan.

"What do you think that will entail?"

"There's a mountain of details I'm sure; I'll find out where to start."

Those tired lines on his face will deepen in the days to come. He must do it all himself.

"You know you'll have the prayers of the other children and me as you do all the footwork by yourself."

"I'll have Mary to help me. She knows what her Dad will go through."

He came back to the bed and held me in his arms.

"I'll have to leave you now for a while; I have lots of things to attend to."

The next day he sank down into the chair by my bed.

"I started out at the U.S. Consulate yesterday; they told me that having the body shipped to the States from a foreign country requires the compliance with some local laws."

"But Mary will be buried by her brother, won't she?"

"Don't worry, Mother, there're just a few obstacles to deal with."

He then filled in the details. The requirement of having Mary embalmed presented a problem. In countries like Costa Rica, they bury people the same day they die so embalming is very unusual. [This was in the 1960s.] Consequently, the cost of embalming Mary was prohibitive; the Consul asked our Ambassador to request a waiver of this requirement. The alternative was formaldehyde. The rest of the requirements presented no problems.

The next day Terry came into the room with tears in his eyes.

"I saw Mary's body today; I told the people here at the hospital that I'd like to see her."

They made a concession for us and placed Mary in the ice house to await her transfer to the funeral home; he haltingly told me that they took him there to see her one last time.

"Mary was lying on a blanket on the ice: a beautiful baby girl with lots of black hair. She looked just like Brigid."

We cried in each other's arms. *How I love this man, the father of my children!* After a while, he continued.

"Mary went to the morgue wrapped in a cloth with formaldehyde; they placed her in a steel container which was then welded shut."

He paused for a while and then added.

"That's a requirement of the law for a body coming into the United States from overseas; it's then prepared for shipment by air freight."

We sat in silence. Then he got up out of the chair.

"I'll have to go to Nicoya tomorrow and get my passport; I'll tell the children then what we plan to do."

We walked down the hall together.

"You won't come here tomorrow then—you'll have to wait for the plane to return the next day."

"That's true; now I'll begin the process of making the arrangements for Mary's and my flight to the States."

As I walked back to my room, I stopped and looked down on the courtyard from the balcony; it was wonderful to smell the fresh air and see the mountains in the sunlight and the flowers in the garden below: It eased the loneliness of the day. After a while, the rain fell, one of those sudden, short, swift showers so common here in San Jose. Then it was breathtaking to look about as the sun broke through again, just like my crying that would start suddenly to relieve the ache in my heart and make it possible to see the beauty again. Looking now, I saw the raindrops on the leaves and flowers in those hushed moments after the shower, reflecting the sun as prisms on a chandelier; beyond them the mountains were dazzling in the fresh-washed atmosphere. Here, by the courtyard, I said the last portion of the Liturgy of the Hours in the evening; later I said my night prayers looking at the low-hanging glistening stars.

Terry walked into the room the next day, much to my surprise.

"I told the pilots that I needed to get my passport; they said they would wait for me so I could return to San Jose right away; I thanked them for their thoughtfulness."

"How are the children doing?"

"They're all fine; they're sad about what happened to Mary but they're happy that I'm taking her to Baby Land by Joseph."

As I looked at him now I could hardly hold back the tears because he looked so tired. Heaving a sigh, he sat down in the chair.

"Well, shipping Mary by air freight's no problem. My going to the States could prove a problem. There seems to be an airline strike affecting passengers but not freight; the airline told me they thought I'd have more options if I went by way of Panama. From there I could go directly to Chicago or New York, and then by train or bus as need be."

He smiled as he shifted to a more comfortable position in the chair.

"There's one bright side to this; remember the wire we received from my brother, Bob, last week? He's in Panama for a meeting and plans to go to Nicoya afterwards."

"I forgot about that. Maybe you can see him in Panama now; that would really help a lot."

"Bob said in the wire he's at the Inter Continental Hotel in Panama; I'll check in the hotel when I get there"

We sat in silence for a while.

"Well, Mother, it's time to say goodbye for quite a while."

"I know."

I held him tightly and tried not to think of what he still had to do by himself.

"I don't know how long I'll be gone; I can't contact you during that time."

"We'll meet the plane every day after a while; may God bring you back safely."

The next morning, Saturday, the nurses woke me at 4:30; I needed to get to the airport in time to catch the 6:15 flight to Nicoya.

"We don't know what to think about you, sneaking out of the hospital at this hour of the day, complete with flowers and suitcase."

"I'm so happy I'm going home to the children."

They helped me into the taxi and I was off.

During the long drive to the airport, the clouds grew thicker and darker. The cab driver turned and looked at me.

"I don't think they'll fly to Nicoya this morning; they don't fly out to the peninsula if it's raining."

"They will today because I need to get home to my children."

When we arrived at the airport, the airline personnel took me to the runway level on the freight elevator. When Terry bought my ticket the day before he had asked them to do that for me. Even though the dark clouds thickened, we took off. Blinding rain greeted us over the last mountain. We made our first stop at Canas. The pilot came out of the cockpit.

"Santa Cruz and Nicoya are closed because of the rain; I'll wait a half hour and radio them again; if they haven't cleared by then, we'll return to San Jose."

I had to think of some way to get home if this plane wouldn't go there; I saw some small, single-engine planes parked here: maybe someone would fly me to Nicoya. I knew the small planes came there when the larger planes didn't.

Our family doctor, Dr. Yockchen, was sitting across the aisle from me.

"Doctor, would you please go into the office and ask them if I could charter one of the small planes to fly me to Nicoya if this plane doesn't go?"

"Yes, of course, I will."

He returned a little while later.

"I'm sorry, Mrs. McCarthy, there's no one here to fly the planes."

I thanked him and rested my head on the back of the seat and told Mary to intercede for me and get me through.

What will the children say when I come home empty-handed? They didn't have the chance to see the baby. I just couldn't bear the thought of returning to San Jose.

Slowly, the rain diminished, and in a few minutes, the pilot radioed Santa Cruz and Nicoya.

He came out of the cockpit. "It's still raining in Santa Cruz but Nicoya is clear! We'll go in to Nicoya and then back to San Jose."

Hooray!

What a beautiful sight. I could see the children now at the airport in Nicoya! The door of the plane opened.

"There's Mommy! There she is!"

As soon as I saw them, I knew everything was going to be all right.

"Let me carry the flowers, Mommy," Sean said.

I'll carry the suitcase," added Cronan.

I couldn't believe only a week had passed since I saw them.

They all said, "We'll walk home, Mommy; Dad made arrangements to have *Senor Coto* drive you home in his Jeep."

The children started scampering off across the schoolyard. *Senor Coto* did not say much as we drove toward town. We crossed the Nicoya River by the saw mill, drove a few blocks through town and back across the river, and up the little hill to the section of houses where we lived.

A big deposit of mud at the end of the sidewalk was clear evidence of the rain Nicoya had earlier in the morning. The neighbor's little pig and chickens scooted noisily back under the fence into their yard as we passed by. A little further, and I walked into our home surrounded by all the children.

"Mommy, we saw Daddy for a while, and he told us all about Mary," said Brigid.

"Did Baby Joe know Mary when she came to heaven?" asked Chris.

"We wanted Mary buried by Baby Joe, too," added Hilary.

Oh, it felt so good to see them all gathered around me.

I looked up at Avelina, standing in the background; she just didn't know how to tell me how sorry she was. She didn't have to say anything: I saw it there in her lovely, dark eyes.

"I'm so glad you had a chance to see Daddy. Yes, of course, Baby Joe knew Mary when she came to heaven. Daddy and I thought you wanted Mary buried by Joe." My answers satisfied them.

Terry, Jr., had done his job well. They all looked great! He proved himself many a time before when called upon, and this was no exception. I smiled at him and then looked at Kevin: what did he have to say? When Joseph died, Kevin, then six years old, didn't say very much about it at the time of the funeral.

About a week later, he stopped on his way up the stairs to bed. "When Baby Joe died, I thought I would die too."

Now he smiled as he looked at me.

"Mommy, we made a baby tenda like the one Daddy and Grampy made when we lived in Grand Haven. We didn't even have to pay for the lumber because when we went to the saw mill, the man said we could have the pieces lying around."

"Bob and I helped transport all the lumber home on our little wooden cart," added Rory.

"Remember when Rory and I made that cart? We wanted it to look like the carts that bring the eggs and bananas to our house," Bob added.

We went into the dining room to look at the new tenda. There it stood, painted white, with the names Brigid, Hilary, and Camille printed on it in black. We had such a time keeping chairs; none held up very long, and keeping enough serviceable chairs around created a problem: Now the little ones had their chair and table combined. So Kevin did this to overcome his sorrow! Tears came to my eyes as I hugged him and the rest of the children. I was so proud of them all. A family's love can absorb such hurt and cushion it to make it bearable.

All of the excitement made me quite tired; I had to lie down for a while. They had the bed ready for me. They went out to let me rest awhile. I lay there thinking about my family. We used quite a few different types of dwellings to house our family in the past couple of years since we left our home in Grand Haven. The family stayed intact, though, and never lost its closeness; in fact, we drew closer.

Right now, the younger ones tried to be quiet; the wooden walls, however, did not extend to the ceiling to muffle the sounds. The same type of wooden wall made up the outside walls too; only screening covered the section near the top; closing doors didn't keep out many of the sounds from the rest of the house or the neighborhood.

I didn't mind it a bit though; I loved to listen to it all. Camille, Hilary, and Brigid peeked in at short intervals to see if everything was all right. Then I noticed the door opening slowly, and Avelina looked in. I motioned her inside, and in her arms she had her 7 month old baby, Jose. Dear Avelina, she knew how I loved Jose, and she went home to get him for me to hold: She let me know how much she cared.

He sat on my lap looking at me with those huge dark eyes; I held him close realizing how attached I was to him. Avelina took off a short time in January when he was born; when she returned, she frequently brought him with her. He got sick quite often; once he had diarrhea, and I offered Avelina the medicine that cured Camille when she had it. She used her own remedy which helped, but it took longer to show results. She did take the medicine to give to Jose at that time; he did very well with it. How I appreciated her thoughtfulness in bringing him to me today!

Sunday morning all the children went to Mass, and later in the day we received a message from Bob: he'd be arriving in Nicoya Monday morning. We hadn't seen him in many years, and the younger children didn't know him at all.

Terry, Jr., Kevin, Rory, Bob, Cronan, Sean, and Chris went to the airport the next morning when the plane came in and welcomed Uncle Bud, as he was known to them. I walked out to meet them as they came up the sidewalk. He looked short walking between Terry, Jr., and Kevin. How they have grown!

It meant so much to us to have him visit at this time. While we sat in the living room talking, a student from the high school asked permission to come in. He wanted to practice his English with us during the recess period. Then we heard Beto Zuniga coming up the sidewalk singing, "Strangers in the Night" at the top of his lungs in his heavy Spanish accent—Frank Sinatra's recording of it was his favorite. He came in, too, to practice his English.

It completely amazed Bob that the students came in like that.

"They do that on a regular basis, Bob."

"In all the time I've spent in South America, I've never experienced that."

"Living so close to the school probably makes a lot of difference."

Bob got up and stretched.

"How about you boys taking me on a tour of your town."

"Yeah, let's go," came the chorus of voices.

I prepared a roast with carrots and potatoes during that time. Now they returned with loads of fresh fruit and a new soccer ball. A huge bowl of fruit salad was added to the menu. Bob's appetite matched that of the boys.

"How in the world can you come up with food like this living here in Nicoya? It's like Mom used to make at home."

"I had to learn how to shop here; I go out early in the morning to the meat market, because they don't have refrigeration. The parts of the butchered cow hang on hooks. I wanted *lomo* (loin) for a roast today so the butcher cut as many pounds as I requested from the remaining *lomo* part of the cow hanging there. He always likes to see me come because I buy pounds of meat at a time when most of the local customers buy only small portions."

"They must have good beef here to have it so tender."

"I cook it all in my trusty Presto pressure cooker just like your Mom did."

"Tell Uncle Bud about the hamburger, Mom," Chris said.

"Well, I tried to get the butcher to grind meat for me; we used a lot of hamburger in our diet at home, and we were hungry for a hamburger. One day he called out to me as I came down the sidewalk: He brought me inside the shop and showed me the large meat grinder he had purchased; now he could grind all the meat I wanted. He called it *carne molino* because it was ground meat and I became known as the *molina senora* from then on."

The next day Bob and the older boys took the bus to Colonia Carmona in the District of Nandayure and toured the road-building and training site of the project. I knew Terry had looked forward to taking Bob on this tour; now it was up to the boys to take him there. Terry, Jr., Kevin, and Rory went there often with Terry so I knew they would do a good job of escorting Bob around the construction site. This new road, cut into the Nandayure Mountains, would give access to the bigger towns for the farmers and ranchers on the other side of the mountain.

Tired travelers came home that evening. Bob said the boys did a good job showing him around. He was quite impressed with the work being done.

We all gathered in the living room after dinner for a last gab fest with Bob. Hilary especially became friends with him right from the start and followed him everywhere he could. The next morning Bob left. He knew how much we appreciated his coming to visit us, especially at this time.

The days passed as we waited for Terry's return; I had not heard anything from him. Each morning, one of the boys went to the airport when the plane came in.

Then, finally one morning, I saw him coming across the schoolyard. I waited until he got to the sidewalk and then ran as fast as I could run, and I was in his arms again. All the pent-up tears came, but everything was all right now. Daddy was home!

"Daddy, Daddy, didn't you hear me?" asked Hilary.

"Daddy, is Mary right by Joseph in the cemetery?" asked Kevin.

"Is there a little bird on her stone, too, just like Joseph's?" asked Terry, Jr.

"Yes, of course. I hear you. Let's all go on to the house now, and I'll answer all your questions.

We said *hello* to all the neighbors standing in their doorways watching us and went into the house. Terry sat down and let the little ones crawl up into his lap and then started answering all the questions.

Looking at him now I could see how much weight he had lost, and how tired he looked. I knew some problems developed at the job site during his absence. He wouldn't get much time to rest. We would do what we could to make it easier for him; I thought of some of his favorite dishes to cook to put some weight on him.

He had much to tell us and we settled down to listen to his story.

"The Consul in San Jose and everyone else helped me in every way they could. They anticipated everything I needed; there were no long lines getting my papers in order or getting what I needed for Mary. The airline gave me a first class seat on the plane to Panama for the regular price.

"Mary departed San Jose on August 19 on Pan Am for El Salvador, Houston, Chicago, and finally to Muskegon, Michigan. I departed San Jose the same day and arrived in Panama a few hours later. Actually I arrived in Panama before I left San Jose, due to a time change. I checked into the Inter Continental Hotel and waited for my brother, who was in a meeting when I arrived.

"I really caught him off guard: surprised to say the least, when he saw me. I briefed him on what had transpired; I also brought him up to date on my project. Between conferences, we visited and walked around town.

"Back in my room, I called Grand Haven to let my relatives know that I was on my way; I called the insurance office in the hope of finding someone more easily. My cousin Mel Camp answered the phone; after some shouting back and forth I did get the message to him that Mary was on her way, and I would follow as soon as possible.

"On the 22nd we were off, me to Houston and Bob to Costa Rica.

"When I arrived in Houston, the strike was over: all systems 'go.' Despite crowded flights, the airlines took me right through; Mary preceded me to the funeral home. I picked out the same little casket that Joe had; I purchased the lot next to Joe's, and I ordered the same headstone for Mary.

"Some of my relatives met us at the cemetery: I really appreciated them coming on such short notice. Within a week's time, Mary came into the world, completed her life's work and took her place by her brother. Now we have two saints in heaven to pray for their brothers and sisters, and hopefully for their ma and pa also."

Terry paused for a while and looked at all of us.

"It's so good to be home again. I missed all of you so much."

"We missed you so much, too; here's a nice cold glass of mango fresco for you. I'll bet you haven't had that for a while."

"That's for sure, thanks."

Avelina came in and welcomed him home. After he finished his drink, he continued on.

"I visited my father and mother, my two sisters, also some cousins, uncles, and aunts in a very short time. Then on to St. Louis to visit some in-laws: I enjoyed talking with them and bringing them up to date on our life in Costa Rica; then back to my home in Nicoya, August 30."

Camille snuggled in Terry's lap, fast asleep. The older boys told Dad about taking Uncle Bud to the job site; Hilary told him about really liking his Uncle Bud; Bob, Cronan, Sean, and Chris told him about taking Uncle Bud on a tour of the town and their new soccer ball he bought them; Brigid told him how much she missed her Dad. Contentment reigned once again in our home: our family was together.

MARY

You came into our world,
beautiful baby girl,
and won a special place
in our hearts.
Your life's work was short
completed in a few hours.
My heart ached as did
my filled breast
with no little mouth
seeking nourishment
to relieve the ache
of both, heart and breast.
You went back to God
how can we not rejoice
through our tears?

Now you and Joe
are our
special intercessors
until we meet again.

Chapter XIII

Confirm Need for My Operation

At my regular six weeks' checkup in September, Dr. Cabezas said after examining me.

"You have an enlarged uterus: it's the size of a two-month pregnancy; it's hard and irregular also, and I strongly advise you to have a partial hysterectomy."

"I know you recommended that when I came here to see you last year because of my heavy menstrual periods. I'll talk it over with Terry and get back to you about it."

After consultation with our doctor in the States, we decided to go ahead with the operation: We scheduled it for October 5 at *Clinica Biblica*. We, more or less, made the same arrangements with Avelina, Maria, and her daughter, Abigail, to help Terry, Jr., Kevin, Rory, and Bob to care for Cronan, Sean, Christopher, Brigid, Hilary, and Camille. Terry's work made his presence at home impossible for any length of time.

A few days before my departure for San Jose, the Annual Report on the contract with USAID was due. Since my job description included secretarial work at that time, I typed the report on a stencil so copies could be made on the machine at the Association Office: I finished typing it the evening before I left.

The next morning I sat at the airport waiting for the plane taking me to San Jose. Terry drove up in the Jeep.

"Here are all the reports; I just ran them off down at the Office; they look good, don't they."

"Just as good as reports can look I guess," I replied as I tried to stifle a yawn.

He kissed me good-bye and started off.

Dr. Yockchen was sitting near me, also waiting for the plane. He said he received a report from Dr. Cabezas informing him of the intended operation.

"Surely Terry's going to San Jose with you this morning, isn't he?"

"I'm afraid that's impossible right now, doctor; he'll come and bring me home."

I arrived in San Jose and went to Dr. Cabezas' office. The receptionist took my information and told me to wait for a while until they were ready to check me into the Clinic. I sat down on a couch in the corner of the waiting room and fell sound asleep. There hadn't been much time for sleep in the past week.

I awoke when the receptionist gently shook me: We were the only ones in the room.

"I'm sorry, Mrs. McCarthy, we forgot about you; we went to lunch. The doctor went into the Clinic to check on you but couldn't find you: We're so sorry this happened."

"Your apology is accepted, so what do we do now?"

"I have all the papers for you to sign and then we will go into the clinic."

I signed all the proper papers and followed her into the clinic.

When I arrived at the assigned room, the bed looked pretty good to me: I crawled in and finished my siesta. In the afternoon, a woman came into the room and introduced herself.

"I'm Ardith Hampshire from San Jose, California; right now I'm working with the Language Institute affiliated with the clinic; I heard you're here alone, so I thought you'd like a visitor."

"That's so kind of you, Ardith—I really appreciate it."

"I brought a book I think you'll enjoy; I learned you lived in Michigan before coming her to Costa Rica: the setting of the book is in Michigan." She handed me the book, *Laughing Whitefish* by Robert Traver.

"Thank you so much for your thoughtfulness, Ardith; I will never forget your kindness."

Later that evening, the anesthesiologist came into the room.

"I was here earlier to give you something to help calm you: I heard they lost you for a while. I thought you might have second thoughts about going through with the operation. As I came down the hall though, I heard snoring coming from the room: You needed nothing to calm you, that's for sure."

"I guess there's an advantage to being busy at home down to the last minute."

Early the next morning they rolled me into the OR for the operation: it was sort of a strange feeling not having anyone around. I had a close relationship with the Blessed Mother Mary, though; I knew she was there with me. Everything went well. As I awoke back in my room, Ardith was there waiting for me. She visited me several times a day during my seven-day stay at the Clinic. She was a very special person!

I followed all the suggestions of the doctor and nurses: First I walked back and forth in my room for a couple of days, then I ventured out onto the balcony, and soon thereafter, down to the courtyard for my walk.

The evening before my departure, the doctor examined me. "You're healed well enough for me to remove the stitches. I'll do that right now instead of having Dr. Yockchen do that in Nicoya."

Terry came to the Clinic October 11 to bring me back to Nicoya; we went to the airport for the 7:00 a.m. flight, but *Lacsa* decided not to go to Nicoya until later in the day.

"Terry, I don't want to go back into the city again. I just want to go home."

"Okay, I'll go look for a small plane that we can charter."

He came back with the news.

"I chartered a plane: we can leave right now for Nicoya."

When we arrived there, the children weren't at the airport: they hadn't heard the C46 come in. Terry and I walked across the schoolyard to our house; I felt a little tired by the time we arrived home.

"It's really quiet here. I don't see the children in the yard."

"They're probably doing their lessons."

Instead we found Chris, Brigid, Hilary and Camille in bed with measles. *Sarampion* it is called in Spanish, too pretty a name for such a bad disease.

Maria, our dear neighbor, was there helping take care of the sick children. Martha Clark didn't want her two children to get the measles so she didn't come to help. Avelina was washing clothes, Maria's daughter, Abigail, cooking. What love they showed us by caring for the children even at the risk of contracting the disease: they didn't, thanks be to God.

Chris, Hilary, and Camille's faces bloomed with the rash; Brigid, however, had a high fever: The rash stayed beneath her skin. That evening I sent Terry, Jr., to get Dr. Yockchen as I still felt a little too weak to go. Brigid lay in the baby bed in my bedroom. Dr. Yockchen walked into the room thinking I had called him to remove the stitches. He stood there for a second; then the other little ones came in: When he saw all the spotted faces, he started to laugh.

"I don't mean to be rude but I just can't believe my eyes; I thought I came to remove your stitches."

"The doctor removed them before I left the hospital; it's Brigid who needs help."

He examined her, opened his bag and gave her a shot.

"I think that will help her get better."

Later that evening all the spots that had been below Brigid's skin broke through and her fever left.

Dear Maria found time to come and help with the sick children. She lived a few houses from us, and I learned so much from her. She was taller in stature than most of the local people. She was poor in a material way, but so rich in character. With eight children of her own, she always found time to patch the boy's blue jeans and sew buttons on their shirts. I loved to see Terry, Jr, Kevin, Rory, and Bob teasing her about the patches she put on their *good* jeans. How she laughed with her eyes sparkling as she answered them. She not only mended the girls' dresses but found time to sew a few new ones.

So many nights I passed Maria's house on the way to our house. (We converted the house that the Murphy family vacated when they went back to the States into an office of sorts. ITAF had a 2 year contract on the houses, so we continued to pay rent on it: That's where I did the typing that Terry needed done.) On those nights that I passed her house, I saw her ironing with only a candle for a light. She always had a big smile for me.

"*Hola, dona Thecla.*"

"*Hola*, Maria. How can you work so late and get up so early to make tortillas, Maria?"

"I can only sleep a few hours and then am awake again: I might as well do the ironing.

In the dry season I would often carry water from the Murphy house in large buckets. When Maria saw me doing this one day, she stopped me.

"You shouldn't carry water like that. It will make your arm muscles large, and you are too fine a lady to have large muscles. You should carry the bucket on your head."

"Maria, the water is much too precious for you to try and teach me how to carry it on my head!"

I liked to watch them carry things on their head though: their posture was beautiful. I could use training like that.

At times when Maria's world fell apart I expected to hear some complaints, but the only noticeable thing was the hurt look in her eyes. Her husband was alcoholic: He frequently became quite violent. The need for her to iron far into the night stemmed from the fact that he ran up a bill at one of the local taverns: She did the washing and ironing for the owner to pay the bill; still she went on with her work, pleasant and calm. Maria and two of the older children did extra work for us and others so the oldest daughter could go to San Jose for a higher education.

"Come and taste the delicious *fresco* Maria brought over!" one of the children would say.

Or, "Mom, taste this fried cake Maria brought us. She calls it *bunuelo*.

She always brought something new for us to try; things she made since she was a young a girl but all new to us.

We insisted that she teach us how to make *bunuelo*; she laughed and said it required much time but she would teach us. The next day she brought over ashes from her wood fire. She boiled two pounds of crude corn with the ashes just as the cooks at *Samara* did when they made the tortillas for the day. I then rinsed it and strained it under her supervision. Then the boys went to work to grind the corn along with one pound of cheese and two pounds of yucca; then they ground it a second time and formed it into patties, fried them slowly, and they were eaten with honey. It was a long slow process but a delicious snack. Maria and her children cooked and ground the corn for their tortillas in the same fashion; now I knew why someone in their family was up at 3:30 every morning to prepare tortillas for the day.

The weeks passed and I grew stronger and soon was back to all my usual tasks. We started gathering information regarding the University of Nebraska's high school correspondence courses for Terry, Jr., another milestone in our lives.

Chapter XIV

Another Thanksgiving and Christmas

By November, the Association for the Development of the Peninsula had only paid a small portion of the amount of money they had contracted to pay when the project started. That money for parts, fuel, and lubricants for the equipment and the food needed for the students in training was crucial. In spite of all efforts to get these funds, none were forthcoming.

The project at that time was inoperative because of the lack of these funds. Consequently, the need evolved to store all the tools and other movable equipment in Colonia Carmona, Nandayure: the last location of the road work. This was the road that went up the mountain from Carmona to Vista del Mar. Terry rented a house in Carmona; he, Terry, Jr., and Kevin took turns staying there with the equipment; they rode the bus because funds for gas and maintenance were unavailable for the vehicles.

Thanksgiving came and Martha and I decided we would forego the turkey part after last year's debacle, and just stick to chicken. It was a very quiet holiday but enjoyed by everyone.

The neighbor to the right of us bought a television set shortly before Thanksgiving. Every evening, their yard and part of our front yard filled with people peering through the front windows of our neighbor's house trying to get a view of the TV screen: Our houses were very close to each other.

The walls of the rooms in our house had wooden cross pieces which held the upright boards, so we had little shelves on which to place things. Terry always took out his gold Elgin railroad pocket watch after work and placed it on the shelf alongside his side of the bed. He bought the watch in Alaska when he worked on the Alaska Railroad while still in his teens. Naturally, he treasured it. The billfold lay alongside the watch.

Thanksgiving evening, I had the bedroom light on for a while and saw many faces peering in our bedroom window while they tried to watch the TV next door. During the night, I awakened with the feeling that someone was in the room. Then I heard the back door scrape and I bolted out of bed and ran to the kitchen. The door was still ajar and I heard someone running down the sidewalk. I started out the door to pursue the person but Terry pulled me back.

"You can't go after them: You'll get hurt."

"How dare they come into our house; your watch is gone and so is the money in your wallet."

"It's not worth getting hurt because of it."

Then I started to shiver as I realized that whoever had taken the watch and money leaned across me to reach the shelf alongside Terry. As you already know, I sleep quite soundly. Maybe it was a good thing I did that night.

We reported it to the police. They thought that more than likely the person took it to sell; however, they said they would try to find the watch for us. Time passed and we heard nothing.

Then one day, the policeman came to the house all excited.

"Here is your watch, *Don* Terry; I saw a man in town with it," and he handed a gold Elgin pocket watch to him.

Terry looked at it closely.

"This watch is very similar, but it is not my watch; there's a little difference in the face; you can return this one to the man you took if from."

"I'm so sorry, *Don* Terry."

"I am, too; thank you so much for trying."

The watch was never recovered.

When we went to Mass the following Sunday, a man came up to Terry and started shaking his hand and thanking him over and over. Terry finally understood why the man did this: He showed Terry the watch the policeman brought to Terry a few days before.

"Thank you, thank you, I just bought the watch in San José; the police told me it belonged to the Gringo whose watch was stolen; thank you for your honesty."

Christmas Eve came. The tree was decorated, the crib in place with the shepherds, sheep, and Joseph and Mary, awaiting Baby Jesus. Terry, Jr., Kevin, and Rory went into town to wait for the bus bringing Terry home from Nandayure.

They returned but Terry was not with them.

"The bus arrived but Dad wasn't on it."

"We'll just wait then; there's nothing we can do."

Hours passed before we heard someone coming up the sidewalk; all the children ran out to see who was coming.

"It's Daddy!"

They ushered Terry into the house.

"I couldn't get to the bus station on time; usually some trucks are on the move but apparently not on Christmas Eve. I finally found one truck going my way and climbed on board."

Now peace and calm returned to the house: Daddy was home. It was time to absorb the wonder of Jesus' birth. We celebrated Christmas Day quietly and happily. On New Year's Day, an American passing through Nicoya heard about the *Gringo* family living up the road; he came by for a visit and stayed the night in the Murphy house.

In early January, I took a few days off to visit Terry in Carmona. He persuaded me to ride our horse, Patricio, up the mountain to check out the new road to Vista del Mar; Patricio knew immediately I rarely rode a horse and took advantage of that: He did exactly as he pleased. He stopped at a house just a short distance up the mountain; no matter how much I urged him on, he just stood there.

Some girls came out of the house and said something to Patricio and gave him a pat on the rump; he took off like a streak of lightening: I desperately tried to stay on him. I leaned forward with my head almost touching his neck, one hand clutching my hat and glasses, the other, the reins, like a jockey on a race horse. We reached the end of the road and he stopped dead still.

I caught my breath and then looked around at the beauty of the scene—it truly lived up to its name *Vista del Mar*, for I saw the Gulf of Nicoya in the distance. When I tried to turn Patricio around he again ignored me for a while and then suddenly turned and took off again: We went flying down the side of the mountain with me in the same position I held on our ascent. Suddenly we stopped and, as I lifted my head, I saw the girls standing there staring at me. They started apologizing and I saw the look of relief on their faces that I had survived. I asked them not to pat his rump again: I'd wait until he decided to go.

At my very cautious urging, he trotted very properly back to the house where Terry waited for us.

"What do you think of the road?"

"Well, from my narrow point of view, I saw the road fly by below me as I lay on Patricio's neck holding on for dear life. The view from the mountain top was beautiful until he turned and flew back: My view of the road in between was the same as my ascent."

Terry's face said it all as he helped me off Patricio.

"Riding horses is definitely not my forte; I think I'll go back home and stick to my packing."

Chapter XV

Preparations to Return Home

Terry attended many meetings during January and February working on alternative plans to resume training. Mr. Farwell sent notice at the end of February that the USAID/ITAF contract would not be renewed in June, along with the notice to inform the Association for the Development of the Peninsula of the 90-day termination of services.

Terry requested permission to work on water resources to fill out the contract. USAID gave ITAF verbal permission to work at spring development. Ed Clark did that type of work in Texas; he knew the cattle ranchers could easily afford this system. Very few supplies were needed to develop a spring; once a spring water system is developed, it should function without maintenance for at least 30 years.

The USAID/ITAF contract then added an amendment to develop spring water for "human and animal consumption," but basically for cattle. The cost involved in building a collection box and trough was under $200 or 1,300 colones. A pioneer program like this needed ranchers willing to invest in the demonstration jobs: One was found on a ranch near Carmona.

Terry and our son, Terry worked with Ed as he developed the spring. An excavation was made into the rock with the water outcropping. The water made its appearance at the bottom of a gully. In an open location, a collection box 6 feet x 8 feet and 6 ½ feet high, for protection during extreme runoff, was constructed.

Within 24 days, natural level was reestablished and permanently maintained. Within another month, the flow rate was well over 3,000 gallons per day. The rancher formerly could keep only seven head of cattle on his ranch during the dry season: The maximum now reached 150 head: The total cost for the system was $135.

This attracted national attention, and a reporter and photographer from the newspaper *La Nacion* in San Jose came to the location. A few days later, a picture of Ed and our son Terry appeared in the newspaper: The headline read, "Modern Moses." The article said Ed struck a rock and water flowed.

Seven springs in all were developed before the end of our contract in June, one of which was for a combination human/cattle consumption spring.

"Moisés" moderno...

ROCAS QUE DAN AGUA PARA LA GANADERIA SEDIENTA

En Nicoya se trabaja actualmente abriendo un ojo de agua para abrevar una finca que carece de abrevaderos en verano. Obsérvese lo imponderable del agua en la superficie sin embargo, al efectuar los trabajos el señor Edward Clark, el líquido constituye a dar en suficiente cantidad para satisfacer un hato numeroso.

Y aquí está la prueba evidente un tanque repleto de agua en forma permanente. En este año sólo había líquido suficiente para tres mil cabezas hoy pueden satisfacer más de doscientas cabezas. En la gráfica aparece el señor Clark acompañado de un miembro del Cuerpo de Paz.

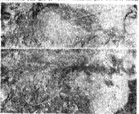

Se ha taladrado la perforación y el agua, producto de la roca, brota como una bendición para los hatos sedientos.

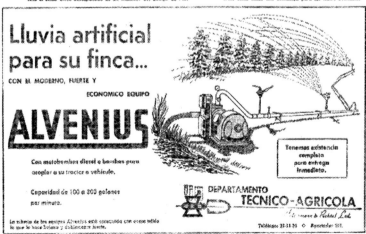

Moises Moderna

At home in Nicoya, we made preparations for our return to the States. We made visits to special friends to say good-bye. We brought out the duffel bags and began filling them.

Terry, Jr., and Kevin decided to take a camping trip with Patricio and Marcia's horse before we left. They planned to go to *Carmona* and then on to *Playa Coyote* which is the beach next to *Playa Samara*. They returned a day later.

"I don't think we're ready for such an undertaking yet," they informed us on their return. "It would take a lot longer than we anticipated."

In San Jose, Terry got all the organizations involved to come up with a contract for Ed Clark to return to Costa Rica for training students in the spring development program: Ed signed the contract on June 20.

The students in the original road program, even though not trained to the degree that we intended, were very successful; some operated farm equipment or other types of heavy equipment; one of the students operated a D4 dozer full time. One of the jobs assigned to him was the road to *Samara*.

On June 18 Terry sent a memo requesting permission for the ITAF group to depart Nicoya on June 28 and San Jose on the 29th. Permission granted.

On June 24, the Association held a small but special farewell party for our family and the Clark family at their office in Nicoya. The *Deputado* (congressman) of Nicoya and the *Deputado* of Santa Cruz attended the party.

A few days later, the school teachers held a party for our families at the school. It featured a group of dancers performing the native folk dance; the most typical Costa Rican dances originated from Guanacaste, a name sometimes given to the Nicoya Peninsula. They wore beautiful costumes. We considered their appearance quite an honor.

The day before our departure, a young boy, a schoolmate of Bob's, came on horseback to visit Bob. Bob came in with a small, white chicken resting in his arms. "Mom, this boy wants me to have this chicken."

My thoughts were far from thinking about chickens at that time.

"Bob, I don't want to buy a chicken now! I'm in the midst of last minute packing."

"But, Mom…"

"Bob, I'm too busy right now."

About a half hour later, Terry, Jr., came in.

"That boy is pretty upset, Mom, because he gave Bob the chicken for a going-away present; he wanted us to have it for our last dinner here; when you said you didn't want a chicken, Bob set it down and let it run away."

I was stunned! I quickly called Bob and his friend into the house.

"I tried to tell you about it a little while ago but you didn't want it, Mom."

I apologized as best I could to the boy and told him we'd all go right out and find the chicken: We went in diverse directions to look among all the other chickens for one small white one.

An hour later with dusk settling in, we met again at the house with Bob happily in possession of the chicken; we didn't dare try to tie it up and take a chance of losing it again. The little boy volunteered to kill it local style by wringing its neck. With that accomplished, we set about heating water on the make-shift kerosene stove, still in operation, to defeather it. Then, under their watchful eyes, I dressed it out, and the first shank was frying away in the tiny frying pan we still had in service.

With that, the boy mounted his horse and, smiling broadly, bid us all "*Adios*". We were very touched that the boy wanted Bob to have the best he had to give before we left: The beds really looked good to all of us that night!

Wake-up time came at 4:00 a.m.; the plane would arrive at 7:00: Last minute packing awaited us. I heard someone outside the door. I opened the door and there stood Maria with a plate full of warm tortillas and sliced avocados to roll up in them.

"Maria, you are the dearest, kindest person in the world!"

She smiled with satisfaction as she saw all of us savor the wonderful breakfast.

How I loved her; she stayed and helped us finish packing.

Then she gave Camille a doll dress she made; she wanted the doll to look nice on the plane. She loved Camille most of all.

We gave Maria the baby tenda that Kevin made for our three little ones: That made her day; she had a little girl who needed it. We took a picture of Maria and her family that morning: She held Camille as though she were her own child.

A small group of people gathered at the airport to say farewell. Tears streamed down Maria's face. It was so hard to leave her.

We spent the night in San Jose; the next day when we arrived at Coco airport, all the taxi drivers lined up to say goodbye. We were on our way to Fort Worth, Texas to begin another phase of our life, stateside.

Ed and Martha Clark, Laura and Catherine, went to Texas with us to visit their folks: They returned to Costa Rica for another year's contract after that.

We arrived in Houston on Pan Am. During the flight from San Jose to Houston, rib eye steaks were served for dinner. We had requested Embassy Travel Division to make reservations at the Carousel Motel in Houston for an overnight stay: When we called the Motel, they knew nothing about our coming.

At 2:30 a.m., enough rooms were available for the sixteen in our group. 6:00 a.m. found us at the Trans-Texas gate for the flight to Love Field, Dallas; we deplaned there, boarded an Eastern jet for the flight to Ft. Worth. It was a 15-minute flight, but it was made in grand style; we had the whole 727 jet to ourselves. We were home again.

We're glad we pursued our dream: It opened a whole new world for us. We made many new friends and new and interesting happenings developed at every little turn in the road: We followed through when we had the chance, and accomplished what we wished to do.

MARIA

How do you say goodbye

to someone like Maria?

Quiet, soft-spoken and loving Maria,

with a smile

that lights up the world.

Not beautiful outwardly as some others

but an inner beauty

that surpasses all the rest.

A woman of genuine kindness

and love that knew no bounds.

Her hard life as the wife of an alcoholic

never got in the way

of her gentle manner,

her love conquered all.

I won't let her go,

I won't say goodbye,

I'll hold her fast in my heart,

She'll stay with me always.

Epilogue

Upon our return to the States, Terry accepted a position at Texas A&M Engineering Extension Service, training heavy equipment operators. Alcoa found him there and contracted him to do that type of training at their bauxite mine in Suriname, South America.

In 1969, when Neil Armstrong landed on the moon, Terry was in Suriname; our children and I followed a few weeks later for another phase of our life in a whole new world.

While we lived in Suriname, our older children began returning to the States for their higher education. All of our children pursued their higher education on their own.

WHERE THEY ARE NOW

Terry, Jr., attended West Texas State University in Canyon, Texas, and graduated with a B.S. in Agronomy. He and his wife, Sue, lived in Bolivia for a time and now live in Tucson, Arizona where he owns a home maintenance and remodeling business. He also directs contemplative retreats as a Secular Franciscan. They have three children, Sarah, Rebekah, and T. J.

Kevin joined the USMC in 1971, and four years later, with the rank of Sgt. rejoined civilian life and earned a two-year degree for diesel engine mechanic. He worked as a mechanic/fabricator/bulldozer operator for a hybrid seed company. He and his wife, Micki, live in Elmwood, Illinois. He now works for a company that manufactures specialized attachments on mining and recycling haulage equipment. They have four children, Carmen, Matthew, Nathan, and Joshua.

Rory attended the University of Missouri Rolla, and graduated in May of 1978 with a B.S. in Geological Engineering. He worked as a mining engineer for Dow Chemical, and then as an Environmental Engineer at Ft. Leonard Wood. He and his wife, Amy, live in Rolla, Missouri, where he now works with Brewer Science, Inc., a semi-conductor specialty chemical manufacturer, as Environmental Manager. They have four children, Ben, Cara, Amalie, and Alanna, and have had 11 foster children.

Bob enrolled at Spartan School of Aeronautics in Tulsa, Oklahoma, and received a diploma in Aviation Electronics. He became a field service representative on C-12 aircraft for Beech Aerospace Services, Inc. (BASI) and moved to Athens, Greece covering C-12 electronics maintenance primarily in the Middle East for BASI and with additional travel to Africa, Europe, Southeast Asia and Australia for them. He, his wife, Nancy, and family lived in Vicenza, Italy for two and a half years and now live in Holbrook, Arizona, with their children Rob, Caitlin, Joseph, twins Gillian and Maegan, Stacy, and Abigail.

Cronan attended Spartan School of Aeronautics and obtained an Associate Degree in Applied Science with an airframe and power plant license. He and his wife, Tina, now live in Colona, Illinois. He works as an aircraft maintenance technician on the corporate aircraft for John Deere Company. They have five children, Louis, Christina, David, who died at age 12 of a rare genetic disorder, Patrick, and Mary, who also died at age 5 of the same rare genetic disorder.

Sean attended Texas State Technical College in Waco, Texas and obtained a power plant and airframe license. He and his family moved to Spain for a few years where he worked for BASI. He, his wife, Dotty, and twins, Kelly and Erin, and Ryan now live in Vacaville, California. He currently works for United Airlines as flight line maintenance controller in San Francisco, California.

Chris attended Spartan School of Aeronautics and obtained an aviation maintenance technician license. He worked in Germany for BASI for four years and then in Honduras for two years where he met and married his wife, Gina. They now live near Portland, Oregon, with their two children, Valentin, and Isabella. He is a mechanic/pilot on a King Air B200 aircraft for a wood products company.

Brigid worked for Burr-Brown, a semi-conductor company in Tucson, as an Engineering Technician. While working there, she also helped an employee with experiments done for a doctorate program. She met her husband, Brian Kram, there, and they now live in Catalina, Arizona, with their children Alisha, Emile, Aaron, Miriam, Kolbe, Aidan, and Agnes. She's a full-time mother and home-school teacher.

Hilary graduated from Northern Arizona University with a B.S. in History with a minor in Earth Science. He has a Secondary Education Certification for 7th through 12th grades and English as a Second Language (ESL) endorsement. He competed in long distance running in high school and college and is still listed in the top ten runners at Pima Community College. He and his wife, Laura, live on the Navajo Reservation where he teaches 7th and 8th grade Navajo and Hopi students. They have two children, Trevor and Aine.

Camille attended Northern Arizona University and earned a bachelor's degree with a major in special education. She taught language arts and reading at a middle school in Gallup, New Mexico, where she met her husband, Duane Smith. They now live in Fargo, North Dakota, with their children, Hannah, Bethany, Veronica, Lydia, and Collette. She's a stay-at-home Mom and a home educator of their daughters.

Breinigsville, PA USA
08 November 2009
227232BV00002B/55/A